W9-CHY-013

Copyright 2020, 2019 Bradley Franc

All rights reserved.

Published by Woodview Publishing Company

THE SUCCESSION SOLUTION℠

The Strategic Guide to Business Transition

By Bradley J. Franc

FOREWORD WRITTEN BY
JIM HOGGATT, FOUNDER & CEO OF EXECHQ™

WHAT PEOPLE ARE SAYING ABOUT THE SUCCESSION SOLUTION℠

Transitioning a business to a new generation of owners is too often a frustrating, confusing, and scary process that ends in failure and resentment. Brad Franc's process is a game changer. A uniquely simple, step-by-step formula that provides a clear path to success for everyone involved.

– *Dan Sullivan,* President,
The Strategic Coach Inc.

Make sure you read this book. I told Brad "Your book is a business survival manual as much as a succession planning tool."

At almost 70 years old I had six of the next generation working in our family construction company - a number who didn't- without a clear succession plan in place. The goal was to pass on leadership from Gen 2 to Gen 3, and have all the stakeholders buy into it! Brad Franc personally led us through a multi-step process using The Succession Solution guidelines to not only develop but to implement a sound plan. It's working, and has alleviated a great deal of stress common in family businesses.

– *Clifford Rowe,* Executive Chairman, Trumbull,
P.J. Dick, Lindy Paving

Building a successful business is a rare and worthy accomplishment. Watching that business succeed into future generations is rarer, and even more worthy. If you own a business you are proud of, then you owe it to yourself, your employees, your customers, and your family to read The Succession Solution℠, by Bradley J. Franc. Throughout the book, Brad not only provides you with a time-tested, step-by-step solution, but also shares personal stories gleaned from his many years of experience. It is a powerful tool for making a difference in your business.

– *Lee Brower,* the Business Family Coach,
Empowered Wealth

The Succession Solution is a must read if you will someday want to transition your business to new leadership and/or ownership. The author, Brad Franc, shares his invaluable experience and knowledge gained as one of the most respected and sought-after succession planners in the country. Brad does so in thought provoking manner and The Succession Solution provides the tools necessary for you to map out your succession plan and begin to execute it. I speak from experience because Brad's book helped me design my succession plan and get it underway!

–*Jeff Holler,* President and CEO,
The Capital Chart Room Ltd.

I love the book. The style is straight forward and logical. It points out the challenge all business owners face, that succession is not a single event. It is a process. The Succession Solution and the work you have done for our company helps owners like us establish policies & practices that align with our values. The Succession Solution may not be easy or comfortable. The best things in life generally happen outside our comfort zone. The Succession Solution is however, very effective. Thank you for taking us outside our comfort zone.

– *Brian Long,* Chairman of Seubert & Associates, Inc.

The process of succession in a closely held business is a particularly difficult. Many factors add to the complexity of the process including divergent shareholder financial goals, varying time frames, family considerations and insecurity in how to proceed. In addition, the shareholders need to maintain focus and commitment to the process while doing all the other things we need to do to continue to have the business thrive.

Brad's proven Succession Solution process addresses all of these complexities in a highly organized, effective manner. Where other programs focus on reports and deliverables, Brad's process focuses on exploring the goals of the shareholders, building consensus and commitment to moving the process forward. This organized and focused process, has allowed our shareholder group to analyze, determine and execute our succession plans.

– *Curt Marsh,* Vice President and General Manager,
Pittsburgh Air Systems, Inc.

Watching thoughtful, highly successful, and otherwise carefully-planning entrepreneurs fail to prepare for the inevitable transition of the company they have nurtured throughout their career, has been one of the biggest unsolved mysteries in my own professional life. Every business owner owes Brad a debt of gratitude for providing a carefully crafted, step-by-step guide that assists them and their advisors in navigating the myriad of questions and options inherent in this process.

– *David J. Malone,* President and CEO, Gateway Financial

Brad Franc hits a home run in the succession planning game. His book provides a soup-to-nuts guide for both experienced estate and succession planners and the business owner. It's apparent that Franc knows his stuff.

– *Bud Smith,* Professor, Katz Business School at the University of Pittsburgh. Author of "Hands-On Consulting".

My Company completed a one year planning period deploying The Succession Solution. From day one, Brad, with the use of The Succession Solution, generated motivation and optimism in regards to increasing profitability and strategic departmental and company-wide planning. The 12 month result was sensational and eye opening to say the least.

– *Robert J. Wade,* President of Wade Heating and Cooling Inc. and Pittsburgh Ductless LLC

We have somewhat of a complex family business and for several years we had the basic thoughts for our estate and succession planning but could not find the right person to help guide us through the process. We found that person in Brad Franc. He took a complex and emotional topic and simplified it for us and encouraged us to simply keep making progress and keep moving forward in reasonable steps until we could achieve our goal of having a comprehensive estate and succession plan completed. Brad led us through this with utmost professionalism and we now have a plan in place that should enable our family business to succeed and continue to thrive and survive in the future.

– *Steven R. Stuck,* President of Stuck Enterprises, Inc.

Having spent the past 25 years in a 75 year old family owned business, I've seen generational transitions go well and thrive, and I've seen them destroy relationships. As a third generation owner, I feel tremendous responsibility to my family, coworkers, customers and suppliers and I realized I'm a caretaker of a wonder asset that takes care of over a 100 families. I have wrestled with how to thoughtfully and properly make sure my business is vibrant and sustainable for the families that rely on the company for their livelihood for many years to come.

Thankfully, Brad Franc has written an excellent book, The Succession Solution, which explains how to transition a business to the next group of leaders. He succinctly, lays out a program that can be followed to give owners their best chance for success. What makes the book so valuable is that Brad has been living and breathing succession planning for closely held company for several decades. Brad's formal training as a CPA and attorney coupled with his entrepreneurial experience and that fact that he's using the Succession Solution with some of the best private companies in the country, makes this book an absolute "Must Read" for every business owner.

– *Scott Heeter*, President of Heeter Printing Company, Inc.

As a practitioner in wealth management for family owned businesses for over 35 years I can say succession planning is one of the most important, difficult and emotionally charged planning steps for an entrepreneur. I have research this topic in depth and this book on the Succession Solution does the best job I've ever seen breaking down an extremely complex subject into a process of actionable steps to achieve value preservation through orderly transfer of ownership and leadership.

Most importantly it systematically breaks through all of the barriers and excuses not to embark on this "mission critical" step required for every family business survive and prosper.

It is a must read for every family member charged with the responsibility to all stakeholders for the orderly transition to the next generation.

I am using the Succession Solution^{SM} for my company!

–*John J. Waldron*, CEO & Founder, Waldron Private Wealth

As a retired business owner and a current Board member, I have experienced firsthand the importance of succession planning. Brad Franc's book shares a powerful message about the importance of succession planning and methods on how to develop, implement and monitor a sound plan. Leaders are the stewards of the future and have the ability to continue to create value to all the stakeholders through creating and implementing a succession plan yet often lack the tools to implement a sound plan. Brad Franc's book provides those tools in an easy to read, easy to understand style that is bound to motivate any leader looking to keep their company running beyond their working years.

–*Joseph P. DiBianca,* Chairman, Global Tax Management, Inc.

We have all heard the horror stories of the hard-working and well intentioned business owner who failed to plan for a successful business succession. If you own a business and realize you need a plan, a path, a playbook on how to transition your business, then look no further. The Succession Solution by Brad Franc is the critical roadmap you've been looking for. This book goes well beyond the technical planning ideas. It provides a straightforward, no nonsense approach to give the business owner a playbook on how to handle, not only the legal issues, but just as important, how to communicate effectively with family members and key employees. He focuses on the goals of all the stakeholders, the ways in which to build consensus and ultimately, and this is critical, a process to manage the succession plan to completion.

– *D. Gregory Steliotes,* President, Innovative Benefits Consulting, Inc.

There's no avoiding it. All viable businesses and their owners will go through a succession process—one that they can either carefully orchestrate and control or leave to chance. The Succession Solution provides forward-thinking owners with a clear process to guide them through this critical work. Brad Franc has hit the mark with a methodology that is both effective and easy to implement.

– *Michael Duckworth*

FOREWORD

By Jim Hoggatt
Founder & CEO of ExecHQ™

After four decades spent offering CEO & CFO consulting services to passionate, successful business owners, there was one thing I saw that concerned me again and again: the resistance these owners had when it came to planning for the eventual transition of their business. Many of the owners I worked with appeared to block this concept out of their mind as they would have at the thought of putting together their will or designing their own burial plans. Others confessed that they saw succession planning as a road that could only lead to the sale of their business. Frankly, it didn't seem to matter how energized they were about their work and the companies they had built, nor how invested they were in the company's future success. Succession planning was a task that was scribbled down far, far at the bottom of their extensive to-do list.

Unfortunately, for many of these owners, this resistance turned to regret later on. I've met more than my fair share of owners who resisted planning or thought they didn't need to do any planning...only to find themselves years later in a desperate scramble to sell their business ASAP after an economic downturn, unexpected family tragedy, or any other number of "bumps" in the road. One example that comes to mind is the story of a self-made entrepreneur who came to me requesting my services after a failed exit strategy led him to lose the company he had built in a series of messy legal battles. Another is the sad story of a past client who founded a successful business of his own and ran it for many years. That is, until he began exhibiting early signs of dementia and convinced himself that he was the only one capable of marketing his business for sale (thus alarming his employees about the longevity of the company and their jobs – and arming his competitors with a reason they could use to convince his clients to work with them instead, rather than with a business that was up for sale and had an unstable future).

While many business owners are inclined to take the "this-won't-happen-to-me approach," stories like the above are a lot more common than we like to think. As Brad emphasizes in his book, the survival rate of a business transition from the 1st generation to the 2nd generation hovers at a measly 30%. The odds get even worse as you transition to the 3rd generation and 4th generations, hovering at 15% and 5%, respectively. And although I had consulted my clients on and utilized strategic plans and exit strategies for two companies of my own, it wasn't until I found Brad's book (recommended to me by a colleague who was so impressed by Brad's message after meeting him that he actually had Brad train and certify him as a Succession Planning Facilitator) that I had a full understanding of all that went into a successful succession plan and why so many of the business owners I met ultimately failed in their transitions.

Here's what made Brad's book grab my attention (and what made it become a staple on my bookshelf that I've since read multiple times). Most books in this industry are focused on the mechanics of selling and exiting a business. Yet, rather than be a rehash of the mere technicalities of transitioning a business, The Succession Solution transcends beyond this by giving readers a practical, 6-stage framework that covers all the critical psychological aspects of succession planning that most businesses forget to think about. This means that, if you continue reading, you'll dive deep into crucial topics like keeping all your stakeholders in alignment, avoiding potential family (or stakeholder) discord upfront, making sure your successors are prepared, and working through common fears and misconceptions about succession plans. And perhaps most importantly of all, you'll get to the heart of why so few closely-held businesses survive a transition and learn how to avoid the common pitfalls they often fall into.

Knowing what I know about Brad, I really don't think anyone else out there could have developed a framework like The Succession Solution and put together this book. Not only has Brad spent the past 25 years counseling hundreds of businesses through their succession plans, but he's also a top-rated attorney, a former CPA, and the founder of multiple fast-growing companies of his own. In other words, he has the technical experience as an attorney and CPA to understand all the intricacies of succession planning, as well as the operational experience of being a founder to understand the actual challenges business owners face as they plan for a transition.

So, if you're a business owner of any kind and at any stage of your succession planning, I recommend you brew yourself a cup of piping-hot coffee, grab yourself something to take notes with, and settle in. The Succession Solution is a fairly quick read (something you can easily get through in a day or two), but reading it will likely be one of the most valuable things you'll do for the future of your business for a long, long time.

– *Jim Hoggatt,* Founder & CEO of ExecHQ™

TABLE OF CONTENTS

Part I:

INTRODUCTION

As a business owner, you face countless challenges, tasks, and tests to keep your business running daily. For many of these challenges, you are already well-armed and experienced. Whether it relates to sales, employees, or the operation of your business, you have been handling these tests for years, and you have a keen sense of how to achieve your goals.

One challenge you may find particularly daunting, however, is the succession of your business. It is a challenge because you may not possess the necessary experience, expertise, or familiarity to do it right. Nonetheless, you must eventually decide what to do with your business. Without an effective plan for the succession of your business, it is very likely your business—along with its value—will diminish, or even fail altogether. Statistics show that approximately 70 percent of all businesses fail to survive past the first generation business owner. More than 85 percent fail by the third generation, and over 95 percent fail beyond that.

Succession planning is an unfamiliar challenge for most business owners. The anxiety of planning is often exacerbated when family members are involved in the business, because then business and personal issues become entwined. Having a plan in place can be extraordinarily valuable. A plan can help eliminate the uncertainties caused by not knowing how to proceed, or help determine what impact succession can have on your employees, family relations, and even your own future financial security.

If you are a business owner, or you are working with one, then this book is for you. It provides both an explanation of the importance of succession planning, as well as a practical, straight-forward, and proven system that can be used to continue your business to the next generation, whether your successor is a family member(s), an employee, or a third party.

This book will show you how to achieve a successful transition of your business to the next generation of leaders. In fact, if you read and follow the steps outlined in this book, you will dramatically improve the survival and prosperity of your company's future.

In addition to the business issues, this book will help you manage the family issues related to your business. Too often, business owners ignore or postpone matters of succession, because they fear unknown family outcomes. However, by providing a roadmap to uncover, address, and manage your family issues, this book fosters the confidence you need to preserve a secure future and focus on growing your business. You will learn a unique and proven process for accomplishing a positive succession plan.

Of course, you may ask yourself: What makes this book so special?

This book differs from other similar books in its ability to navigate your step-by-step journey through the successful transfer of your business to the next generation of managers or owners. By following the steps listed in each chapter, you will ensure your own financial well-being, while also ensuring that you have left your business in the hands of competent leaders who will develop and improve your employees and add value to their family's lives.

While many business owners are frequently excellent entrepreneurs, they sometimes don't possess the tools necessary to develop or appreciate the impact of the succession plans they build for their companies. As a result, they naturally turn to their existing advisers for counsel. However, those advisers are often ill-equipped to see your entire situation. Advisers can only provide you with what they know.

Business owners have often told me that they regretted where they ended up with their succession plan. Too many times, they did not plan for the result they obtained. Too many times, they thought following the counsel of a tax adviser or attorney would result in the correct succession plan.

Unfortunately, too many times, business owners follow the advice of a CPA or an attorney who may mean well, but is swinging a 900-pound tax hammer, and as the saying goes, when you're holding a hammer, everything looks like a nail. As a business owner, you want to take a broader view with your succession plan.

Missteps and oversights occur for any number of reasons. For instance, you may think everything will take care of itself, or you may want to wait a little longer before you find the right person, or you will let the tax tail wag the dog. Maybe you trust that the next president or Congress will solve your problem. Business owners have told me they regret taking their adviser's recommendation to gift a substantial amount of assets to their children in the name of tax planning.

I think the main reason business owners end up with an undesired succession result—or, worse yet, their business fails—is because the business owner does not have a process to use to address major concerns. This book provides you with that process by taking a broader approach to your succession plan and helping you focus on more than just saving taxes or keeping a certain relative out of your company. In fact, following this unique process will allow you to design, test, and apply the various ideas and strategies presented by your tax, legal, and financial professionals. You can then determine if a particular strategy moves the business closer or further away from your desired destination.

If you decide to start a succession planning process, you should commit to seeing it through. I have witnessed business owners create more damage to their family or organization by developing a plan and then ignoring it, instead of not planning at all. The process described in this book will help you avoid this dilemma by providing a system that is easy to understand and work with. I have distilled the succession plan into a single but powerful one-page tool I call "The Succession Solution^{SM}."

Why I Wrote This Book

Several years ago, I attended an educational program in Manhattan specifically developed for attorneys, financial planners, and CPAs who practice in succession planning for closely-held businesses. The program presented the leading experts in the fields of business law and taxes. Many of the program topics covered specific Internal Revenue Code (IRC) sections and specialized techniques that tax and legal providers could deploy to transition a business to the next generation.

While some of the speakers effectively communicated their topics, there was one attorney from New York City who said something that set me on my course to support closely-held business owners in the transfer of their businesses. This presenter began by offering some startling statistics: only a third of businesses succeed to the second generation, and fewer than 15 percent make it to the third generation! Then she hit me, along with the rest of the audience, with something none of us expected. She asked, "Do you know whose fault it is for such a high failure rate?"

There was complete silence in the room; it was as if we were all expecting an answer to the meaning of life. She responded to her rhetorical question by announcing to the crowd that it was *our* fault. Yes, our fault. She stated that as professionals we had failed our clients by not emphasizing the importance of succession planning and explaining how to do it.

To be honest, I don't ever like to believe something is my fault, but after some reflection, I knew she was correct. We attorneys, CPAs, and financial planners were not doing as good a job as we could be doing in assisting our clients with succession planning. I think we get too involved in one particular transaction or technique of succession planning, and we forget about the process as a whole, and the need for concerted action. In other words, we lose sight of the forest for the trees.

I have found that succession planning consultants, advisers, and professionals typically fall into two distinct camps. In one camp, we have the technical wizards who show us how to avoid taxes and prevent creditors, mostly in-laws, from touching our hard-earned businesses. In the other camp, we have the psychologists and professors who explain the interpersonal challenges of succession planning. Few of them seem to be able to provide a practical framework or process which incorporates the business, family, and technical aspects of succession planning.

I realized that if I could incorporate all of these elements of succession planning into one process, I could assist business owners in their succession plans. I would also be supporting the employees, their families, and even the community impacted by the company as well. This book is the result of those efforts, and it is why I have dedicated my professional career to assisting businesses with their succession plans.

Who Am I to Write This Book?

In over thirty years of working in this area, I have counseled hundreds of closely-held business owners on their succession plans. I have been named by Worth Magazine as one of the top one hundred attorneys in the United States. I have published several articles, presented to various business groups all over the country, and have appeared on national television and radio on succession planning. Some of the tax articles I have published have been cited by the United States Supreme Court to help decide tax law.

Also, I bring a number of different disciplines to the table that few other professionals can offer. First, I began my career as a CPA for what is now known as EY. As an auditor, I gained a great deal of knowledge about the financial aspects of both small and very large companies. Once promoted into the tax department, I acquired a deep understanding of the Internal Revenue Code.

After working as a CPA, I went to law school and finished at the top of my class. During law school, and for the past thirty years, I have worked in a law firm representing closely-held businesses in succession planning. For several years, I was the president of the law firm, which was one of the top twenty largest law firms in Pittsburgh, Pennsylvania.

During my tenure, we experienced our own succession challenges. Also, during that same time, I encountered many clients struggling with similar challenges when planning for the successful transfer of their businesses. Clients ranged from majority owners/CEOs, to minority owners, to in-laws of minority owners and to disgruntled next generation family members, just to name of few.

I formed a total of four companies over the last twenty-five years and was fortunate enough to have them named nine separate times among the fastest growing companies in the USA by *Inc.* magazine.

I led the quarterly strategic planning meetings for twenty-five years, and I am confident it was our commitment to strategic planning that led to accelerated growth across all four companies. We identified and encountered our own succession planning issues, including shareholder disputes over dividend distributions, compensation, and naming the next CEO. As the saying goes, necessity is the mother of invention, and it was during this time that I developed The Succession Solution℠ as a way to strengthen my own companies.

If You Decide to Take the Leap

The Succession Solution℠ will guide you through identifying and addressing the concerns of your important stakeholders (including yourself), while helping you design the best overall plan for your company. Not only will you have a plan in place for new and competent leaders to take over, but you will be able to demonstrate to the new team the importance of succession planning. You'll have added confidence, knowing you have fulfilled the responsibility of your leadership role by taking the company through the important task of succession.

How can I make such bold statements? Well, as I've said above, my conclusions are drawn from years of first-hand research. I have tested and demonstrated this process with remarkable results. My experience developing a unique succession solution process can be compared to the story of the internist, Barry Marshall, who in 1981 came to realize that stomach ulcers are caused by a particular bacterium and *not stress*, as so many of his colleagues believed. For Marshall, it was clear that to heal an ulcer, one needed only to treat the bacteria causing it. Unfortunately, the medical community discounted Marshall because he was young, inexperienced, and, worst of all, an unproven intern without an ulcer-curing credit to his name. How could this young, unknown, and unproven intern possibly have the cure for ulcers? Unable to convince the medical community of his theory, Marshall ran an experiment on the only human patient he could ethically recruit: himself. He drank the bacteria he believed caused ulcers, and after becoming very ill, he biopsied his own stomach! Because of his determination and courage, Marshall unequivocally proved that a specific bacterium—not stress—was the underlying cause of ulcers. Because of this young doctor's beliefs and actions, the healthcare community dramatically changed how it treats stomach ulcers.[1]

Although I am a little older, and it has taken me a little longer than Marshall to run my experiment, I am happy to report that the processes outlined in this book have proven to be effective, not only for my own companies, but for the many other business owners I have worked with. The Succession Solution[SM] is a map to help you determine precisely what you want to achieve with your succession plan, as well as how to identify and avoid the hidden traps that may stop you along the way.

My Promise

Following the steps outlined in *The Succession Solution*[SM] will dramatically improve the prospects of your company's succession to the next generation. You, your family, your company, and its employees will be in a more secure position to compete and prosper. You may even discover hidden opportunities as you go through the process that would not otherwise have presented themselves.

Part II: Succession Plan Foundation

CHAPTER ONE: GETTING STARTED

"Your life doesn't just 'happen.' Whether you know it or not, it is carefully designed by you."

– Steven R. Covey, *Seven Habits of Highly Effective People* (Habit 1: Be Proactive)

Throughout history and cultures, effective business leaders have developed and implemented their own succession plans. One such example is the Japanese traditional inn Hōshi Ryokan, which was formed in 718 A.D. and continues today. Some thirteen hundred years and almost forty-six generations later, this beautiful inn represents the oldest family-owned business in history.

The current owner-manager of Hōshi Ryokan, Zengoro Hoshi, and his wife work in the business every day. Zengoro states that he has two all-important purposes for the inn: first, to provide hospitality for its clients, and second, to prepare for succession to future generations. Zengoro's business philosophy is to "study the water running down a small current." The water continues to improve the stream by removing small obstacles on its way.[2] This simple but powerful philosophy demonstrates the importance of continuous improvement toward a goal, and it can be applied to succession planning. Succession planning is not a one-time event. Rather, it is a process that will create continued improvement in your company.

For over a thousand years, the Hoshi family has deployed its own unique model for succession planning, based on the premise that only one heir will inherit the family business and name. This centuries-old model may work well for those family businesses that wish to transition family assets and reduce potential business risks resulting from a constantly growing family. For others, though, this model may not work. The central goal of this book is to help you find your unique process for an effective succession plan.

What is Succession Planning for the Closely-Held Business Owner?

I view succession planning for the closely-held business owner as the (i) development, (ii) execution, and (iii) subsequent review and adjustment of a plan to transfer your business or position to the next generation of either managers or owners. The next generation may consist of family members, hired professionals, employees, or an unrelated third party in the sale of your business.

Succession planning consists of three essential parts. The first part is the plan itself, and it should be designed to accommodate your particular situation. What do you want your design to look like and why? The second, and equally important, part is the execution of the plan. As author Joel A. Barker said, "Vision without action is merely a dream. Action without vision just passes the time. Vision with action can change the world." This is how you must look at your succession planning—as active, even visionary, engagement.

The third and final part involves the review and adjustment of the plan. Like a plane that takes off for a particular destination but must adjust along the way, your succession plan must be flexible enough to adapt to the unpredictable, real-life contingencies that can affect your business.

A Relay Race

An analogy to consider with succession planning is that of a relay race. When I ran track in high school, I learned that there is a process involved in a relay race. A relay race is not about any one person; it is about the team, and while it is important to have the right team members, the overall objective is to win the race. It's the same in business; a company should never be about any one person, but the business itself.

One of the most vital parts of a relay race is the handoff of the baton. Some of the greatest runners in the world have lost because of a bad handoff during a relay race. As the business owner in charge of your business, you are holding the baton. It is your job to run your portion of the race as best you can. To be successful in this role, however, you can't just think about running fast, or about the baton handoff, or how fast the guy in front of you is running. Instead, you must consider *all three.*

Succession planning works the same way. You must consider a number of issues and follow a specific process to achieve the successful transition of your business. As with a relay race, if you focus on one thing only (like saving taxes or keeping certain family members happy), the chance of a successful transition diminishes. Any effective succession plan process should help you keep your eye on the critical issues and milestones necessary, so you can successfully pass the baton and win the race.

The Succession Solution℠ is a step-by-step process that guides you through clearly defined steps before taking specific actions and/or making any final decisions. If a business owner goes through each of the defined stages of the succession plan, the likelihood of success increases dramatically.

What about this elevated confidence we mentioned in the introduction? The Succession Solution℠ generates confidence in four primary ways:

1. When you follow a defined and proven process rather than making a rash decision, you know you have addressed the important issues in your business and personal life.

2. The process recommends that you seek input from other key stakeholders (aka "relay runners"), which increases the likelihood that others will support, adopt, and even help implement the plan.

3. Going through the process often reveals hidden opportunities or positive outcomes that you would not have otherwise considered.

4. Performing the process on a quarterly basis allows you to continually assess your progress and readjust the plan to meet and achieve your goals.

The Five Ws and How of Succession Planning

While I am passionate about the importance of succession planning, I do not recommend you proceed with any succession planning process unless and until you consider the fundamental elements of succession planning, including the risks as well as the benefits. As a business owner, you must understand or see what you are getting yourself into before you begin.

In his book *The Back of the Napkin*, best-selling author and management consultant Dan Roam outlines a very powerful but simple process to examine as well as explain almost any problem or situation.[3] Roam explains that while there may be a vast quantity of ways in which to examine and describe a problem, all are derived from just six basic concepts. If you consider these six concepts you can analyze and understand practically any situation more clearly.

The six fundamental concepts described by Dan Roam are sometimes referred to as *The Five Ws and How*. I have found *The Five Ws and How* to be useful for understanding almost any complex situation. The phrase stands for: What, Why, When, Where, Who, and How. You can address just about any issue with this approach, because it allows you to understand a situation by looking at it from almost every angle. In fact, the *Five Ws and How* technique, with its basic question-and-answer format, has been used for centuries by entrepreneurs, institutions, and even religious orders for information gathering and problem solving.

We'll discuss each question in detail, but here is a summary of the six questions proposed by *The Five Ws and How* to help you better understand the stages of your own succession plan:

1. Why do you want to take on this succession planning project?
2. What should take place during the process?
3. How should it happen?
4. When should you begin and what are the timelines you'll agree upon?
5. Where should the process be conducted?
6. Who should be involved in the process?

Now let's go through each question in detail.

1. Why do you want to take on this succession planning project?

This is the most important question you need to answer before you embark on any succession plan. Once you've identified the "*why*," you can then begin to develop the purpose for your succession plan. Without a clear purpose, your chances of success are limited, because it is the purpose of your plan—the core of your why—that will give you the reason to carry on.

For example, your why may be that you want to see the business continue for key employees who have been with you for years. Or maybe you want or need to extract the value from the business in order to better enjoy retirement. Whatever your *why* may be, it is important to define it so that you have a reason to proceed.

The answer to your why delivers the much-needed incentive to complete the process of building an effective plan. Moreover, when conflicts arise during the process—as they are apt to do—your why will provide the support and guidance you'll need to confront them.

Let me give you an example. Let's imagine you are struggling with selecting one of your children to succeed you as the president. You are concerned about the impact this decision will have on your other children. If you have already developed your purpose for the succession plan, it often becomes less difficult (not easy) to make the decision, as well as explain the decision to everyone involved. Your purpose may also lead to the development of a process which allows you to address a conflict by agreeing on how best to deal with it from both a business and family perspective.

Another very common answer to the why of succession planning as a business owner is to establish financial security for you and your spouse. Obviously, you are one of the most important stakeholders in this process. A closely-held business is often the most significant part of your retirement. You may look to your company for some form of buy-out or retirement package. Consequently, to ensure a healthy retirement, your company must survive. Without going through a succession plan, you may be uncertain if you can retire and still be financially secure. Knowing that the question of when you can retire is your why allows you to go through the succession process with the clear goal of determining if you can retire now or if you need to postpone the retirement until certain agreements are in place.

Another important reason to answer the why is to inform your advisers, who will be assisting you. Your advisers will likely play an important role in implementing your succession plan. If they understand your why, they will be better equipped to help you with the process.

2. What should take place during the process?

While answering the why is the most important first step, your *what* is the most comprehensive question to be answered. After determining why you want to pursue a succession plan, you then move on to what you should expect, plan, and strive for in the specific succession plan you develop.

What do you want your succession plan to achieve? Will you expect a plan with action items to be identified and delegated to specific individuals? Ask yourself, “What do I think an effective succession plan will look like when I am done?”

An example could be the development of a specific plan that outlines the date you will transition from CEO to chairman of the board. It might list who will be the next CEO and how it will be announced to the company and its customers.

Typically, determining the *what* involves a process in which sufficient time and resources will be set aside for all stakeholders to express their views, so they can be heard, respected, and considered. The plan you develop should also contain objective goals, as well as include a process to measure and report back to the group both the details of the process and/or any recommended changes to the plan.

You will also want to include a record-keeping system that measures and reports the process and changes to the plan that can be easily read by all members of the group.

3. How should it happen?

This question addresses how to start your succession plan. There is no specific way to start, but there are some best practices for how to go about developing and deploying a succession plan. How you decide to proceed can impact the success of your plan. The Succession Solution℠ process is designed to answer this question.

Before you schedule any meeting or retreat to discuss implementing a succession plan, solicit the individual opinions of your important stakeholders. Important stakeholders can consist of members of your board of directors, officers, key employees or family members. A key stakeholder is anyone who you view as important to your company and could be impacted the succession of your business.

Let them know what you are thinking about and ask for their input. Do they think a formal succession plan should be developed? Do they have any ideas about what should be discussed or not discussed? Do they have any thoughts about who should attend or not attend? Would they like to be included? What do they think are the most important issues to discuss?

Once a determination is made to proceed, ensure that all the stakeholders you want at the meeting agree on the date and are able to attend. It is very important that all key players agree to attend the meeting, because without one important person, much of the meeting's effectiveness can be lost.

Along with ensuring everyone can make the initial meeting, you'll want to confirm that everyone is scheduled for follow-up meetings. I recommend you meet quarterly. Such a commitment shows your team you are dedicated to the process, and they are more likely to be engaged when you demonstrate your own fidelity.

Next you will decide whether or not you want to engage a third-party facilitator. Employing a professional who is proficient in this area is beneficial for two reasons: First, a third-party facilitator will act as the historian of the meeting. He or she will be the one responsible for taking notes and recording the plan. Second, the facilitator will act as a dispassionate and objective participant during the meeting. A good facilitator will help keep the meeting professional and respectful, which will prove invaluable when and if the meeting becomes emotional.

As an example, I facilitated a meeting with a family planning the retirement of the majority shareholder, CEO, and patriarch. The gentleman had a successful business and had previously transferred stock to each one of his three children, solely for tax avoidance. During the succession planning meeting, an issue arose concerning the daughter, who was not working in the family business. The young woman was resistant to sell her stock back to the company in order to allow for a concentration of stock to be held by the sibling who was working in and leading the business. After a protracted discussion, the father continued to question the daughter as to why she would not sell her stock, and it was clear she was becoming extremely distraught.

Finally, the daughter shouted at her father, telling him she was still upset because twenty years ago, when she had wanted to enter the business, he had told her it was no place for a woman. The father, however, had completely forgotten about this conversation. When I intervened to ask the daughter what she wanted to do, it became clear that she was not interested in keeping the stock, but she did feel it was important to address how her father had made her feel so many years ago. Because we took the time for the daughter to explain herself, her father was able to offer his sincere apology. Had I not been there to step in at the right time, the situation could have escalated, and the process could have broken down altogether.

A facilitator can also keep the meeting on track. If you don't have a third party acting as a sort of traffic cop, some folks will get on a "soapbox." In these situations, a third-party facilitator can control the clock and make sure everyone is heard equally.

Whenever I am involved in a succession planning process, I sit down individually with each participant before the meeting and let them know what to expect. I also set basic ground rules regarding cell phones, meeting breaks, and participation. Again, the more you plan in advance, the better chance you'll have of achieving a smooth overall process.

4. When should you begin and what are the timelines you'll agree upon?

When to begin the process is dependent upon your individual situation. It is never too early to begin your succession planning process. Ask yourself the question Dan Sullivan, creator of The Strategic Coach program, likes to ask his clients – The R-Factor Question®: If we were sitting here five years from today, what would have to happen with respect to your succession plan for you to feel happy with your progress? If your answer is, "I don't need to do anything; I have it covered," then it is not the right time to begin.

If your company is fortunate enough to have a functioning board of directors, the board should encourage starting the succession planning process. This is a fundamental role of the board of directors. Board members should be able to state exactly what would happen if you are unable to perform your duties.

While some succession plans may take longer, if you are within five years of some form of succession, I recommend you begin the process. As they say, "the best time to plant a tree was twenty years ago. The second-best time is now."

Let me reemphasize that once you begin the process, you'll want to plan on meeting on a quarterly basis.

5. Where should the process be conducted?

You may choose to meet at your business, but there are benefits to meeting off-site at a comfortable location. Meeting in your office allows for too many distractions, whether it is a customer who wants to speak to you or a colleague with a "quick question." No matter how big or small, these distractions will disturb the meeting, and they can be viewed as a sign of disrespect to everyone in attendance. Selecting an off-site location allows complete focus, and it will ensure that attention is directed only at succession planning and everyone involved.

Finding a nice location does not have to mean expensive. Any comfortable location where people can get up, move around, and feel relaxed will do. Promote the meeting as a positive gathering and choose an environment that accommodates that effort.

6. Who should be involved in the process?

Once you decide to act on your succession plan, the next step is to decide whom you will invite to the planning process. While it is possible to complete the succession planning by yourself, I strongly recommend that you consider inviting others—it can get lonely out there!

Typically, the folks you want to consider inviting are any major stakeholders who will be most impacted by the succession plan. You may not end up inviting every significant stakeholder to the planning session, but it is important to identify them now so that later you can refer back to them during the succession planning process. Furthermore, you will want to make sure that, while you are developing your succession plan, you have considered the impact on all identified stakeholders.

Don't think, however, that just because you've identified important stakeholders, you must now tailor your plan to accommodate each of them. Rather, you must understand how the succession plan will impact these stakeholders, and how your plan will address their needs. You will face challenging decisions during the planning process, but if you keep your major stakeholders in mind, you will be better prepared to make those decisions.

The people you choose to invite to the planning process will be critical to its success. I have found that it is better to err on the side of more rather than less inclusion. However, it is good to remember that just because someone is listed as a major stakeholder, it does not necessarily make them a qualified participant; if that person does not understand or acknowledge the importance of the succession planning process, then they should be excluded.

Another reason to invite some or all of your major stakeholders is to garner their acceptance: stakeholders are more likely to accept a plan they are involved in creating. When you invite an important stakeholder to the planning process, you share ownership in the succession plan. A sense of inclusion often leads to a willingness to participate and collaborate to arrive at a common goal.

What Succession Planning is Not

While there are different parts to a succession plan, often a business owner is advised of a particular technique which he should employ to solve a particular succession plan issue. But, by adopting a specific technique or tactic, he fails to address other important aspects to his succession plan. Here are a few common examples of elements of succession planning which by themselves do not constitute a succession plan:

> **1.** A succession plan vs. an estate plan: Succession planning is not the same as your estate plan. While your estate plan can certainly have a huge impact (positively or negatively) on your succession plan, it is not a substitute for your succession plan. Typically, your estate plan will consist of a last will and testament (will), a power of attorney (POA), and a living will. Your will directs the legal transfer of all the property in your name. Therefore, if you own stock in a closely-held business at your passing, your will directs who will own that stock. If you don't have a will, the state in which you reside will then direct the transfer. The second document is the POA, which is a very important document, but not a substitute for a succession plan. The POA names an agent to act on your behalf in the event you become incapacitated due to an illness or accident. An

agent under your POA essentially steps into your shoes from a legal perspective and is empowered to act on your behalf. Without a POA, if you become incapacitated, your family will likely have to go to court to have you declared incapacitated, which can be costly and time consuming. The last document is the living will, which deals with end-of-life decisions. As you can imagine, a living will is certainly not a substitute for a succession plan.

2. Succession planning is not exit planning: Exit planning is the process of planning for your exit from the business, rather than the succession of your business to the next generation of leaders, owners, or managers. Exit planning is often focused on the sale or liquidation of your interest in the business. Although a succession plan may eventually result in the sale of your business, the focus is much broader, encompassing the continuation of your business and the goals of important stakeholders, including your own.

3. Succession planning is not tax avoidance: There may be effective tax strategies and tactics you can deploy to save taxes in the transfer of your business, but the reduction of federal or state death and income taxes should not be the primary focus or driver of your succession plan. Before you begin a discussion about tax planning with the succession of your business, you should first decide why and how you want your business to be transferred. Only after you decide on your succession plan should you discuss the tax strategies. Don't make the mistake of allowing the "tax tail to wag the succession dog."

4. Succession planning is not creditor protection: Creditor protection can be an important part of an estate plan or succession plan, but it should not control your succession plan. I often hear business owners express anxiety and concern over their company falling into the hands of a disfavored or divorced in-law. Many advisers will default into forming a trust to protect stock or assets from creditors, only to regret it later due to the restrictive nature of trusts. Succession planning takes a broader view in the transition of your business. While creditor protection can be part of your succession plan, there may be more critical risks and threats to address.

Next Steps

There are many reasons why businesses fail to continue from one generation to another. For instance, a business can fail due to family discord, the lack of an adequate leader, taxes, or a liquidity crisis at the passing of a founder. A lack of planning is rarely the cause of failure, but proper planning and implementation can be the solution, the remedy, or even the antidote to the problems that can destroy a business. If properly executed, your succession plan can help you find your succession path, as well as address any underlying problems to provide a much greater chance for the survival of your business.

If planning is so effective, then why do so many business owners fail to plan? There is no single reason why business owners avoid planning. The key question to ask when considering your succession plan is, "What *might* be holding me back, or what *is* holding me back from succession planning?" Once you identify the reason(s) behind your resistance, you can begin to make progress. Once you overcome your hesitancy, and commit to proceeding, you will be well on your way to creating a successful plan.

You also need a system and a structure to follow when undertaking a succession plan. Consultants and advisers may come in and develop a beautifully-designed plan, complete with mission and vision statements, but then they leave the rest up to you to complete. While you may develop an effective succession plan, there must be a system or process in place to execute on that plan, or it will fail.

Developing a plan and then ignoring it can cause more damage to your organization than never developing a plan at all. Often a company will gather a large group of smart executives or family members in a room. The gathered members will generate a number of great ideas. Someone will take notes and the famous long-form plan will be developed, consisting of 15, 20, or even 50 pages, and all sorts of charts and graphs. The results will then be distributed to everyone engaged in the plan, and if the company leaders are proud of it, they may even share the plan with all the employees to showcase how wonderful it is.

The problems arise only afterward, when the plan is ignored. When one person brings the plan up for discussion, another might comment that there are more pressing issues to deal with. Once that statement is heard too many times, no one wants to raise the matter again.

The answer to this dilemma is to find a process where you can efficiently develop and implement a plan that can be understood and employed. Of course, no succession plan will address every minute issue, but the plan should address the material issues you face and install a process to revisit your plan.

If you complete most of your plan each time you meet to work on it, you'll soon have a project that is just about perfect! Too often, we get caught up in the details, and we don't realize the importance of the process itself. I believe in progress, not perfection. I also believe that the process moves more quickly and effectively with momentum.

I challenge you to ask yourself a question: "If I could accomplish 80 percent of what I desire in my succession planning, would I view it as a success?" If your answer is yes, then continue reading.

Keys to Chapter

1. Succession planning is the (i) development, (ii) execution, and (iii) subsequent review and adjustment of a plan to transfer your business or position to the next generation of either managers or owners.

2. The next generation may include family members, employees, hired professionals, or an unrelated third party in a sale of your business.

3. The specific written document you select is not as important as the process itself, and a well-thought-out plan of succession is far stronger than a plan of inaction.

4. Seek progress and not perfection when implementing your plan.

CHAPTER TWO: TAKE THE SUCCESSION SOLUTION^{SM} ASSESSMENT

"We can't improve what we don't assess."

– Michael Hyatt

The Hénokiens Association is an association of family businesses that have been in existence for more than 200 years. The association takes its name from the biblical character Enoch, grandson of Adam, who was said to have lived 365 years.

In order to become a member of the Hénokiens Association, a company must meet four criteria: a member must have reached a minimum of 200 years in existence; the company must be managed by a descendant of the founder; the family must still own a majority of the company; and the company must be in good financial condition.

So how do these companies survive for over 200 years? In April of 2015, the *Economist* published a special report on family companies[4] and researched the Hénokiens Association. The *Economist* found that even though the member companies increased the number of owners, they were able to avoid significant family disputes by operating under an agreed-upon set of rules for how the family and business would interact, including who could own shares and how ownership could be transferred. The conclusion was that long-lasting family businesses survive by following written plans that address the ownership and management of their family businesses.

I have also found common elements among business owners who have successfully transitioned their companies. While your business may possess its own unique circumstances, there are common fundamental best practices that should be in place to improve your chances of success to the next generation. Even though your company may not install each and every "best practice," you can gain insight by comparing your current situation to those developed by others. The Succession Solution[SM] Scorecard will help you do just that.

An Assessment Tool for Succession

A few years back I participated in an educational program with several other professionals, including financial advisers. During a conversation with one adviser, she asked if I had heard of the estate planning assessment tool she'd been using with her clients. She explained that it consisted of a list of questions concerning the participant's estate plan. Once completed, the questionnaire would provide an overall score and make suggestions for areas of improvement. Since I had not heard of the assessment tool, she asked me to review it and provide my opinion as to whether I would recommend its continued use for her clients. She also asked if I would take the assessment myself, and if I would mind sharing my score with her. I should have figured she was setting me up!

Feeling rather confident that I would naturally score in the assessment's top ten percent, I completed the estate planning tool (you might guess where this is going). To my surprise and professional embarrassment, I received a score of 75 percent, and when I shared my score with the woman who recommended the test, she encouraged me not to feel too badly, because I'd actually scored better than most.

My score may not have been terrible, but I could not shake the feeling that something had gone wrong. I decided to carefully review the questions and the overall report. After close scrutiny, I realized the assessment had exposed a number of areas in my own estate plan that needed improvement.

I share this anecdote only to provide you with another lesson on the importance, not just of planning, but of periodically reviewing your plan to ensure its continued effectiveness. Even when you think you have the best plan in place, a careful review of that plan can produce valuable insight.

I believe in the value of a good assessment tool, but I want to stress that you adopt a data-informed rather than data-driven approach to your succession plans. While statistics and data are valuable tools to be used for guidance and direction, they should never dictate or control your every business (or even life) move.

I developed The Succession Solution℠ Scorecard to help you understand and assess your own succession plans. This assessment tool is for those of you who want to determine where you fall in the continuum of succession planning. I have pared the scorecard down to a list of the top twenty-five questions you ought to ask yourself, your team, and your family. Once you complete the process, the scorecard will provide two important insights.

The first insight is the actual score, which supplies a context for how your succession plan compares to the plans of other professionals I have worked with and researched. While this score is not the definitive answer to whether your business will succeed to the next generation, it will offer insight into how your succession plan stacks up against others.

The scorecard's second insight rests in its ability to reveal those areas in your succession plan that need additional focus. By highlighting potential trouble spots, the scorecard acts as a diagnostic tool for determining the health of your plan. As Peter Drucker, famed management consultant has said, "If you can't measure it, you can't improve it".

I have worked with many successful business owners over the years, and I am often amazed by what they have accomplished and continue to achieve. What is less encouraging, however, is to see how underprepared these powerful captains of industry can be when confronted with their own succession planning process—even those who are part of multiple generational businesses. As a result, many business owners are uncertain as to how prepared they really are for the succession of their companies. The situation highlights the old adage, "I don't know what I don't know," but it doesn't have to be this way, which is why I developed The Succession Solution℠ Scorecard.

If your succession score falls in the lower range, there is no need to panic. Rather, you can use this score as a baseline to determine your progress as you proceed with your succession planning process. In fact, the scorecard's results will show you how well you are doing and give you the confidence to proceed further with your plan.

If your succession score falls in the high range, congratulations on your fine work. However, I would still challenge you to proceed through the full plan. I have often found that improvements can be made with even the most prepared business owners and plans (including my own!). In fact, I have found that business owners who have already made progress with their succession plans are eager to continue with their improvement.

Before proceeding to the next chapter, take the time to complete The Succession Solution[SM] Scorecard on the following page, or online at www.thesuccessionsolution.com/scorecard. Not only will it help you identify the state of your current succession plan, but it will also highlight any areas you need to work on as you move forward.

SUCCESSION SOLUTION SCORECARD

Score each question with the number that best reflects the answer.

1	2	3	4
STRONGLY DISAGREE	SOMEWHAT DISAGREE	SOMEWHAT AGREE	STRONGLY AGREE

1. You have identified a date when you would like to transition or relinquish control of your business. ______
2. You have calculated a value for your business. ______
3. You have talked with your family about the succession of your business. ______
4. You have a written succession plan in place for your business. ______
5. You have identified a specific successor for your business. ______
6. Your identified successor is motivated and prepared to assume your role in management. ______
7. You have identified who will receive the ownership of the business. ______
8. Senior management is in place to operate your business in the event you are unable to do so. ______
9. If there is more than one owner of your business, then a written agreement is in place to address the transfer of ownership. ______
10. You are not personally liable on a bank debt or to any business creditors. ______
11. You have calculated the death taxes, expenses, and other costs that will occur at your passing. ______
12. Your estate has the liquidity to pay the death-related expenses in the event of your passing. ______
13. Your business has no bank or other debt which becomes due at your passing. ______
14. You have an estate plan that reconciles with your succession plan. ______

15. You have a Power of Attorney that addresses your business. _____

16. Your business and the rest of your estate can be divided fairly (as determined by you) among your family. _____

17. The business has a defined dividend policy. _____

18. No family members wish to own or work in your business. _____

19. You have a family employment policy. _____

20. You have a competent team of professional advisers (CPA, attorney, etc.). _____

21. You have decided how you will transfer ownership of your business, either by gift, sale, or other form of transfer. _____

22. You have developed your personal goals for after you leave your business. _____

23. You know how much income/assets you will want before you exit from your business to maintain your lifestyle. _____

24. There is a consensus among your key stakeholders over the current succession plan. _____

25. You have an active board of directors involved in the succession of your company. _____

Total _____

SUCCESSION SCORECARD

0–60 .... Significant risk of failure of succession to next generation.

60–75 .... Potential risk of failure of succession to the next generation.

70–85 .... Significant progress has been made, continue the good work.

86–100 .... Congratulations, you're set to have a strong succession plan in place.

To complete this scorecard online, visit **www.thesuccessionsolution.com/scorecard.**

Keys to Chapter

1. A good assessment tool will allow you to benchmark and improve your succession plan.

2. An assessment tool is meant to be used for guidance, but it should not dictate your plan.

3. According to Peter Drucker, "If you can't measure it, you can't improve it."

CHAPTER THREE: WHAT SIDE OF THE STATISTICS WILL YOU CHOOSE?

"All we want are the facts, ma'am."

–Jack Webb, as Joe Friday

While it may not be determinative to your situation, being aware of the statistics on the survival of a closely held business is important for every business owner. I will illustrate with the story of Alexander Sanguigni, who started a business that made him a nineteenth-century immigrant success story. Over time, the business Alexander worked so hard to build turned into the all-too-common American succession story: shirt sleeves to shirt sleeves in three generations.

Alexander was born into a humble but hard-working family in Pisa, Italy in 1880. At the age of nine, along with his two sisters, he came to the United States with his father, Francesco, and his mother, Maria. Francesco and Maria sold everything they owned before leaving Italy. Life expectancy standards in the United States in 1900 were less than fifty years,[5] so both Francesco and Maria, who were in their early forties, were considered relatively old for such a bold move.

The Sanguigni family settled in Pittsburgh, Pennsylvania, residing in a tenement building with other Italian immigrants. Alexander's father was a baker who decided to start an Italian bread and macaroni trade. Over time, the bakery business prospered and employed several members of the family.

All while driving a delivery truck for his father's bakery business, Alexander took on a variety of jobs to help out, from bicycle repairman, to cook, to auto mechanic. One day, while on a delivery for the bakery business, Alexander met Anna, a young woman who had also come from Italy when she was only eight years old. Shortly thereafter,

Alexander and Anna married.

After their marriage, Alexander continued to pursue a number of businesses with some success. During this period, Alexander and Anna were rewarded with a family of nine children, four sons and five daughters. Eventually, with his truck delivery experience and knowledge of auto mechanics, Alexander bought a used delivery truck. He wasn't aware of it at the time, but Alexander was about to embark on a journey that would culminate in the realization of his entrepreneurial dreams: the creation of a family trucking and excavation business, A. Sanguigni Sons Company.

The company flourished under Alexander's direction, growing into one of the largest excavation companies in western Pennsylvania. Alexander also contributed his time, talents, and resources to a variety of community and sporting events, and a community park named in his honor still exists today.

The Sanguigni business thrived even through the Great Depression, but then, in 1939, Alexander passed away unexpectedly at the age of fifty-nine, leaving everything he owned to Anna, including the business. Anna was suddenly left to figure out what to do. She was one of Pittsburgh's first court interpreters, and she was a smart woman, but she had little experience in the construction trade. Nonetheless, at the age of fifty-eight, and with nine children ranging from twenty-two to thirty-eight, Anna had to decide her next move. Some of the children were already working in the business, while others had chosen separate careers.

Without the necessary knowledge, Anna was uncertain what to do. The business not only provided her with financial security, but also several of her children and a host of other employees as well. Anna knew she would have to decide quickly. She knew that if she waited too long, the business would likely diminish in value. In the construction industry, a large value of the business is often based on the relationships developed by its president or owner. Without Alexander, Anna needed to find someone with the skill to take over the family business. She needed to find the right successor, and fast.

In an effort to be as fair as possible to each of her children, Anna decided to permit each family member to submit a sealed bid to buy the company. Presumably, she knew only those experienced in the business would or could enter a sustainable bid.

Although her oldest son, Richard, was steeped in the construction trade, Anna expected he would not bid on the business because, at that time, he was affiliated with the Seabees, the construction division of the U.S. Navy. Although Richard felt a strong sense of responsibility to his family, his loyalty to his country influenced his decision to remain in the armed forces rather than return to the family business.

In response to Anna's request for bids, her other son, Camil, submitted the successful bid to buy the entire family business. Camil was thirty years old, and like his oldest brother, he had the skills to take over. Camil proved to be an outstanding successor to his father, and the company flourished under his expert direction.

Over the years, Camil grew the family business by working on some of the most important construction projects in Pittsburgh, including the excavation of the iconic Three Rivers Point Park. As his father Alexander had done, Camil continued the family tradition of contributing to the community with the company's time, talent, and resources.

Unfortunately, like his father, Camil passed away unexpectedly at the age of fifty-six. Unlike his father, however, Camil did not leave the business to his wife. Instead, Camil's Will left the business to his two sons to decide how to proceed. The two sons soon realized they could not work together. One son decided to leave the family business to work for another construction company. The remaining son stayed to run the business. He attempted to buy out his brother's shares in the company. When the two brothers were unable to reach an agreement on price or terms, the brother who remained in the business decided he did not want to run a business where fifty percent of the profits went to a non-working family member. As a result, he decided to liquidate the company by selling the existing equipment to third parties. Thus, the family business of A. Sanguigni Sons Company came to an end at the start of the third generation.

The fate of the Sanguigni family business is just one example of the all-too-common American succession story that has been repeated for generations. A young entrepreneur starts a company and with its success is able to support his family, employees, and community. Fortunately, in the face of an unexpected challenge, the A. Sanguigni Sons Company business made it to the second generation, due in large part to the selection of a terrific successor. However, when the same challenge faced the company a second time, the company did not survive.

What ultimately caused the failure of the Sanguigni family business? How does one of the most successful excavating companies in Pittsburgh fail to continue when it is passed on to the next generation? Was it because one brother did not want to share the profits with the other? Was the brother who remained in the business not competent enough to run it? Why did one brother abandon the other so soon after their father's passing? Could any of these issues have been addressed prior to Camil's death?

The end of the Sanguigni business resulted in a number of losses. The company's employees lost their jobs, the community could no longer depend on and benefit from the company's generosity, and finally, the end of the business meant the loss of a family legacy. Due to the lack of a clearly-defined succession plan, the business that Alexander Sanguigni created was lost forever.

I don't know if the failure of A. Sanguigni Sons Company could have been avoided, but I do believe that their chances for success could have been improved with a better plan for the succession of the company. Could Camil have anticipated and addressed the possibility of sibling rivalries? Could he have better trained and educated his sons to run the business? Could he have divided the business into separate companies for each son to run? These are some of the tough questions all business owners need to ask and resolve.

You're probably wondering how I know so much about A. Sanguigni Sons Company. Well, Alexander Sanguigni was my great grandfather, and it was my grandfather, Richard, who decided to serve his country in World War II rather than come home to bid on the family business. While the company had already ceased to exist during my youth, I often heard my family members lament and question why such a successful company had been lost.

Like most business succession stories, A. Sanguigni Sons Company's history had its own unique facts, but its ending is all too common, and it demonstrates why you must learn from both your failures and your successes.

World-Wide Phenomena

Failure in business succession is not unique to the United States. Rather, it is an international occurrence. The worldwide belief that wealth corrupts has resulted in the development of many language phrases. Below is a list of popular aphorisms about succession planning from various countries:

1. From peasant shoes to peasant shoes in three generations: **China**
2. Father-merchant; son-playboy; grandson-beggar: **Mexico**
3. Who doesn't have it, does it, and who has it, misuses it: **Spain**
4. The first generation creates, the second inherits, and the third destroys: **Germany**
5. From the stable to the stars and back again: **Italy**
6. Rice paddies to rice paddies in three generations: **Japan**
7. The father buys, the son builds, the grandchild sells, and his son begs: **Scotland**
8. Shirtsleeves to shirtsleeves in three generations: **USA**

These popular sayings are evidence that poor succession planning is a human condition not related to one particular country or nationality.

Important Facts and Statistics About the Closely-Held Business

One reason to study statistics is to learn the likelihood of a certain occurrence. Statistics do not guarantee an outcome, but they often indicate the tendency of a result. Accordingly, use statistics as a tool rather than allow yourself to be controlled by them, or assume a certain outcome will occur.

There is much research and data on the closely-held business which you can use in the development of your succession plan. An understanding of the facts surrounding the succession of a closely-held business will equip you with the knowledge and tools to build your own plan. Aside from the facts unique to your situation, there are often many common elements in successful and not-so-successful plans.

In its most basic form, a business is defined as closely-held when a small group of shareholders controls the operation and management of the firm. Evidence shows that most closely-held businesses are family-owned.

Closely-held businesses are the lifeblood of the United Sates, as well as the global economy. Almost two-thirds of the world's wealth is driven by family-owned or closely-held businesses. One-third of the S&P 500 is comprised of family-owned businesses, and according to many studies, over 90 percent of all businesses in the United States are closely-held.

According to recent IRS census figures, there are approximately 6 million corporate tax filers each year, and only about eight thousand of them are public firms.[6] As you can see, there are far more closely-held businesses in the United States than publicly held. Closely-held businesses are vitally important to the economy: they employ 48 percent of the labor force (2018 Small Business Profile Office of Advocacy). According to a 2013 Forbes report, family businesses generate over 50 percent of the Gross National Product (GNP) in the United States.[7]

It is clear from the facts that the closely-held business is one of the main engines of our economy, tax revenue, and national employment.

Survival of the Closely-Held Business

According to the Family Business Institute, from generation one to generation two, there is a survival rate of approximately 30 percent, and the survival rate continues to worsen from the second generation to the third and even to the fourth generation. Statistics show the survival rate drops to less than 15 percent from generation two to generation three, and then further by the fourth generation where the survival rate is barely three percent.[8] In other words, 70 percent of all businesses fail to survive past the first generation, with over 85 percent of all closely-held businesses failing to make it to the third generation; the vast majority of all these businesses will not be around in fifty years.

Illustration 3.1

Success Rate Between Generations of Closely-Held Business Successions

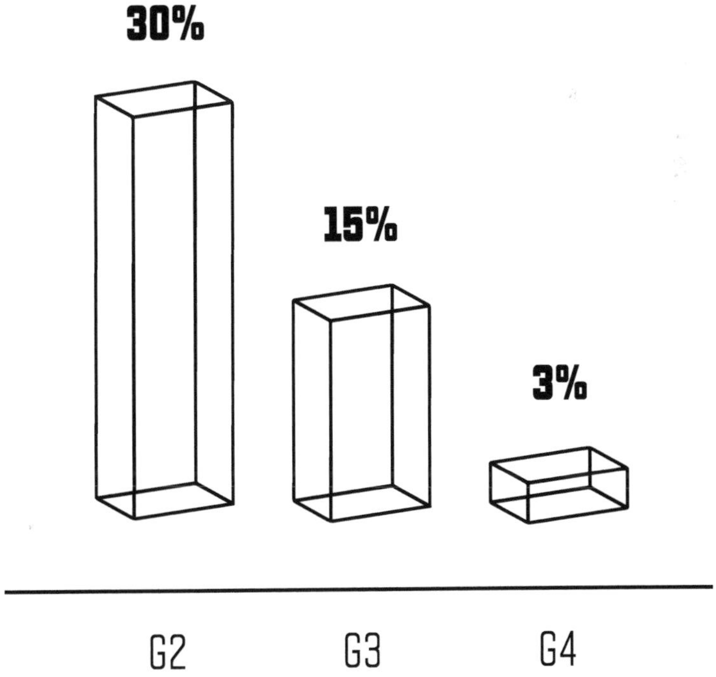

Surprisingly, most business failures are not the result of poor estate planning or taxes, but rather non-technical issues within a business owner's control. For their book *Preparing Heirs*, Roy Williams and Vic Preisser interviewed 3,250 families that had transitioned a family business or significant wealth. From their study, the authors estimate that 60 percent of transitions fail due to lack of family communication and trust among family members, 25 percent due to failure to adequately prepare heirs to manage wealth, and only 15 percent due to technical wealth planning.[9] See Illustration 3.2, Reasons for Unsuccessful Transitions.

The terms "communication" and "trust" are further defined by the authors of the study. Effective communication means the ability to speak openly and honestly concerning information sought by other family members. Successful families are able to have difficult conversations because they know the result will be much worse if no discussion occurred.

The term "trust" does not mean dishonesty or some other deceitful purpose. Rather, trust is given to someone who is reliable, sincere, and competent. In other words, it determines if a family member can be trusted to complete a task, or if they could be relied upon to complete what is assigned to them. Where there is a lack of trust, families will seek alternatives, which often causes confusion and conflict among family members.

Remarkably, this means that 85 percent of all family business succession failures are within our control and not caused by external forces. In other words, the inability to resolve family conflicts and train the next generation of leaders is the overwhelming cause of succession failure.

The authors also identify three differences between successful and unsuccessful transitions. The successful transitions include the following: (i) total family involvement, (ii) a process to integrate that family involvement, and (iii) the learning and practice of skill in the areas of communication, trust, accountability, articulating and sharing of common values.[10]

Total family involvement includes both the parents and heirs in the group that discuss what should happen in the transition. While this type of family involvement may prove to be more time consuming, and sometimes more challenging, it yields more successful transition results.

The second element found in successful transitions involves a process that integrates the decisions of the family. Methods are adopted and deployed that incorporate the family's values and principles. The authors state that "there needs to be an overarching, proven process that will keep everyone on target, translating their individual wishes into a consensus leading to specific...instructions and actions."[11]

The third element involves the teaching and learning of basic communication and values that are important to the family and business. The successful family knows what is required, and it requires those skills be practiced, used, and demonstrated.

Failure to Plan

In their 2017 annual survey, the international accounting firm PWC indicated that only 23 percent of surveyed business owners have a documented succession plan.[12] Even though more than 50 percent of business owners indicate a change in ownership will occur in the next five years, over 75 percent of them have not developed a plan to accomplish this challenging task.

The statistics are not much different for Canada. According to a Canadian Federation of Independent Business survey, small and medium-sized enterprises have not adequately prepared for their business succession. Only 8 percent of owners have a formal, written succession plan; 41 percent have an informal, unwritten plan; and the remaining 51 percent do not have any succession plan at all.[13]

And my favorite business succession planning statistic is that 100 percent of all business owners will leave their businesses, whether planned or not planned.

Based on the statistics and research, what can we learn about achieving a positive succession? While there may be no silver bullet to this challenge, one very powerful route that has proven effective is the adoption and implementation of a sturdy succession plan. Again, as the authors of *Preparing Heirs* indicate, one of the important elements of a successful transition is the adoption of an established process and action, like The Succession Solution^{SM}.

The proof is in the actual process. Even though there is a 70 percent failure rate of succession, practically every business owner I've worked with who chose to follow The Succession Solution^{SM} approach successfully transferred his or her business to the next generation. In each situation, we developed a defined written game plan, executed on that plan, and adjusted as needed.

It is important to reiterate that lack of planning is not the underlying problem. Rather, planning can help you solve the problem by following a process to (i) identify the problem, (ii) decide on a plan to solve the problem, and then (iii) execute on your plan. If you take the time to develop and implement a plan, you can confront the single most important challenge the majority of business owners avoid, and increase the chance of survival for your business significantly. Further, if you include the next generation of stakeholders, you will be teaching them the values of your company and letting them know what will be expected of them.

Illustration 3.2

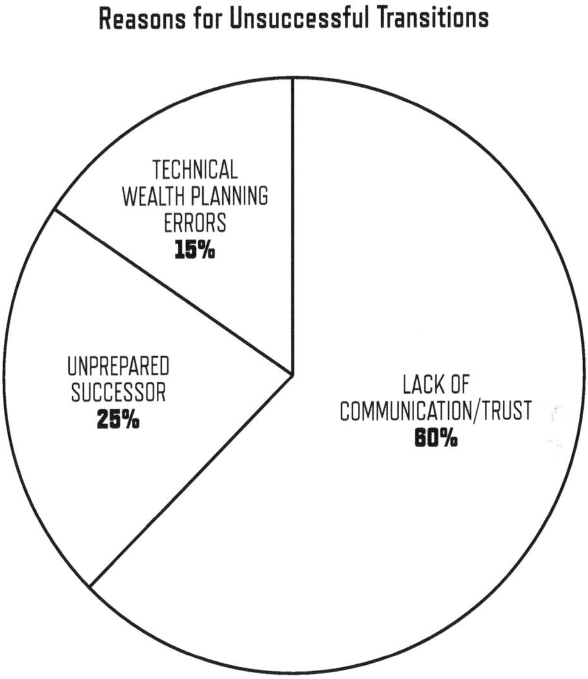

The Economic Value of Succession Planning

The Boston Consulting Group found that implementing a succession plan led to a material difference in the revenue growth, market cap and EBITDA (earnings before income, taxes, depreciation, and amortization) of the company. (EBITDA is a common calculation to determine the value of an enterprise.) The consulting group also found a reduction in EBITDA when an unplanned succession occurred.[14] It is clear from this study that there are significant financial benefits from effective succession planning.

The economic value of succession planning was also evidenced in a 2015 study by *Strategy+Business* of publicly-held companies. The study showed that companies in the highest performing quartile exhibit characteristics of good succession planning practices. In fact, those top performing companies developed succession plans 79 percent of the time. In contrast, the companies in the lowest performing quartile exhibit the poorest succession planning characteristics and corresponding practices.

Using the Statistics

Knowing the statistics related to succession planning can be a powerful tool for designing your individual plan. These numbers reveal overall success as well as failure rates of succession for closely-held businesses. When you dig a little deeper, you discover that this information proves invaluable when deciding how best to proceed. These statistics can be powerful insight for you to recognize that your succession dreams, if not articulated in a defined plan, can be undermined if you don't identify the obstacles preventing the achievement of your plan, and decide how best to address those obstacles.

Knowledge of the staggering failure rate of many closely-held businesses is what initially drew me to focus on succession planning in my work. I was shocked when I first learned of the outrageous failure rates of many closely-held businesses. I could not believe so many businesses fail from one generation to the next. I felt there must be a way to improve this rate of failure. One of the first steps I can help you with in the design of your succession plan is to arm you with the facts. A clear fact is how stark the numbers can be when business succession is left to chance.

If you are like most business owners, you seek the facts to support the transaction under consideration before you make any important business decision. For instance, if you want to open a new store in a new market, you do the research to determine if there is a demand for the enterprise or if the market is already saturated with competitors. If you are about to hire a high-level employee, you require a resume and perform a proper vetting process. Because fact checking is a solid and common business practice, this chapter provides some fundamental facts related to closely-held businesses, and the realities surrounding the succession or transfer of those businesses.

Performing a risk analysis is a familiar step undertaken by business owners at the beginning of any strategic planning processes as an attempt to identify the risks associated with any new venture.

As a successful business owner, you know that having the facts about a situation helps you make strong decisions. While it is true that you will never design your succession plan based solely on what you know about other succession failures or successes, it is important to understand what typically happens (and why it happens) when other business owners undertake the succession planning process.

Of course, there are times when you must "go with your gut." But given the choice, you would likely choose more information over less. As with all things in life, you need to balance the knowledge you gain from facts and statistics with the specifics of your own unique situation when making decisions.

Keys to Chapter

1. Closely-held businesses are not only the lifeblood of the United States, but also of the global economy. Almost two-thirds of the world's wealth is driven by family-owned or closely-held businesses.

2. Seventy percent of all businesses fail to survive past the first generation. The survival rate worsens from the second generation to the third. Statistics show the survival rate drops to less than 15 percent from generation two to generation three.

3. Eight-five percent of all family business succession failures are within your control and not caused by external forces. The inability to resolve family conflicts and train the next generation of leaders is the overwhelming cause of succession failure.

CHAPTER FOUR: WHY CLOSELY-HELD BUSINESSES STUMBLE IN PLANNING

"One of the things we often miss in succession planning is that it should be gradual and thoughtful, with lots of sharing of information and knowledge and perspective, so that it's almost a non-event when it happens."

– Anne M. Mulcahy

A few years ago, I worked with a true rags-to-riches entrepreneur. This man started out selling used cars. Eventually he came to own a number of extremely successful car dealerships. When I asked what made him so successful, he mentioned the lessons he learned from his father, but it was what he said next that really surprised me. He told me that there were just as many lessons from his father that he wanted to repeat as the ones he didn't. Coming from a challenged family myself, I could not agree more.

Too many business books highlight a few successful companies or outstanding executives. These examples are used to illustrate a particular system for achieving success, or to prove specific theories. The element missing from these books is the lessons that can be learned from business failures, which can be just as educational—if not more so—than the successes.

While success stories can show you a path to or process for achievement, looking closely at common failures can alert you to the potential landmines you want to avoid as you proceed.

Survey of Business Owners

As part of my research for this book, I conducted a survey of closely-held business owners who were members of YPOI (formerly known as the Young Presidents Organization), an international organization of business owners. I asked the members, "If planning is the most effective approach to a successful succession, why do you think so many business owners fail to plan?"

Below are some of the replies I received from business owners all over the world:

1. At the very core of everything, long before planning, is letting go. Letting go at a very deep and profound personal level. I think many equate their succession with an ending rather than a new beginning.

2. For sure, planning is an essential step. But there's one step that must precede it: planning to plan. This requires overcoming resistance; accepting that succession means change and change can be painful; recognizing there's lots of data to gather and that task may be overwhelming; accepting that equal may not be fair; acknowledging that not everyone affected by the process may be pleased with the result. There are challenges to overcome, like the fear of hurting someone; having one's personal and family life enmeshed with the business; not knowing what to do next in life; being reluctant to ask for help from one of the abundant professionals trained, experienced, and skilled in the process.

3. In my experience, the most common gap families that claim to desire multi-generational wealth face is their ability to reliably execute on the things that "we" know work. The entire suite of systems, structures, and processes are known (just pick up any of the family business books out there—they universally recommend the same things that promote continuity).

4. Simple reason: it is scary for most. It is not in their expertise. Their business is their expertise, and it is easy to stay in that place. Family dynamics are hard. The concept of "fair" cripples many closely-held, mostly family, businesses. Being "fair" destroys most businesses and many relationships.

5. One of the most common habits business owners avoid is working ON their business. They get stuck working IN their business. Most have lousy strategy, if any. Most do not have a deep bench which limits how they allocate their time. Successful companies build their bench. Successful CEOs work ON their business.

6. I think many people don't plan because they don't want to have the hard conversations. And they don't want to do the hard work. It is tough to run a business and complete succession planning. For example, we have a family council meeting on Monday to hopefully move forward on some issues. It is time consuming, creates some conflict, but it is necessary to be successful. Sometimes we are good at running our business but don't know how to do the succession stuff.

7. Because there is seldom a clear proven capable successor at hand.

8. Ownership transitions are unique to the business and to the family. The outcome is forged or destroyed in a merciless crucible. Very few succeed, because it requires the ability to depersonalize and to personalize at the same time in the right amounts in the right order amongst everyone involved.

9. We think we're immortal—or at least we think transition is "way down the road," so we don't need to plan that far ahead. Often that is correct (other than as a contingency plan—like writing a will), but we get so used to thinking we don't need to worry about that now that it becomes a permanent state of mind.

10. You are asking people to plan for their own obsolescence. Many entrepreneurs and family business owners have a disproportionate share of their identity wrapped around what they do. This is what gives them the most personal satisfaction, and it requires the business operator to face a bunch of demons around the question of "What am I other than my business?"

11. Sometimes succession planning requires making difficult choices between competing family members. We would rather avoid that topic than risk ruining a family relationship.

12. Sometimes succession planning requires facing up to the fact that family members aren't and never will be willing or able to assume the reins. While it is easy to objectively say they're perfectly fine with that, it can be a tough pill for the operator or family members to swallow.

13. We may fear that doing this sort of planning will create uncertainty, which will hurt the business—even if that is not true.

14. Too busy running the business and making money to worry about that.

15. I think people don't do succession planning because of ego. They assume they are the best person to lead the company and think perhaps that no one will be good enough to take their place. (This is unlikely, of course, but people do think this way.) Especially in a family company where family, business, and occasionally power lines can get blurry, succession planning can be messy, because everyone thinks that their son or daughter is the best option.

16. I would imagine because it is hard and complex is why most families procrastinate. Also, it is effort typically required on top of the "day job." At the core, there must be a genuine desire by the previous generation to see the legacy continue, and the successive generation to share the same desire.

The Top Ten Reasons for Resisting or Failing to Complete Your Succession Plan

While each business has its own set of unique facts, my experience demonstrates that the reasons most succession plans fail are relatively limited. Your ability to identify your own specific rationale for avoiding succession planning is critical to future success. Once you pinpoint the reason(s) holding you back, you are free to address them and make progress. I have found that you can't address what you don't acknowledge, so here are the ten most common reasons that hold many back from getting started:

1. Conflicts inherent in your family business. As mentioned, succession planning experts have stated that more than 85 percent of all conflicts over succession planning involve the family. Ironically, a family crisis is more likely to occur when the challenges and problems associated with your family's involvement in your business are not addressed. It is not surprising that when faced with the complex tax, accounting, legal, and operational issues associated with succession planning, tackling family issues can be the straw that breaks the camel's back. Given the added complication of navigating family issues, it is no wonder you go into "shut-down" mode and do nothing.

2. Fear of the unknown. Human beings are not always rational, and because the consequences of succession planning are not readily seen, you move the issue to the bottom of your to-do list. The succession process can evoke strong emotions, being often connected to retirement or death, which can push you into the realm of the unknown.

For some of you, your position of authority has served to fortify your identity, and you don't want to let go of control. Indeed, you may feel no one can do as good a job as you can.

Or you may fear initiating a succession planning process will upset family dynamics, which is emotionally unsettling. You may be uncertain as to who would be your best successor, or there may be more than one family member in your business, and selecting one member over another may negatively impact family relationships.

In these situations, failure to initiate a succession plan can have dramatic effects, both on your business and your family. Postponing the process can leave others anxious. Trying to guess who your successor will be or when they might (or might not) be selected can create even more strain in your family than going through the process itself.

3. Too long or complicated. Quite often, well-intentioned and competent advisers will develop very sophisticated succession plans that may indeed save on taxes or provide great creditor protection. The problem occurs, however, when the plan becomes too complicated or takes too long to be implemented. In such cases, you can become overwhelmed by the depth and breadth of the plan, and when a proposal becomes too difficult to implement, you "conveniently" forget it. I have had numerous clients come to me with mountains of succession planning paperwork, only to admit that they have no idea what it all means.

The elegance of The Succession Solution^{SM} is in its simplicity. It is designed to be easy to follow and understand.

4. Too many advisers saying too many different things. Many of you have competent legal counsel, CPAs, bankers, and financial advisers, and when you meet with them, they offer sincere counsel on how and why your business should go through its succession plan. Problems arise, however, when the advice of one professional conflicts with the advice of another or is inconsistent. In these situations, you become frustrated and might cope by just ignoring the recommendations.

This is why I advise engaging a single adviser whom you trust and respect to captain the process. Because it is crucial to have the advisory group working together, this team leader can be tasked with ensuring everyone understands each professional's distinctive advice. Too often, an important aspect of your business plan gets lost in translation. With a team leader, each adviser will be reading from the same game plan, and there will be less confusion.

5. No time. According to Stephen Covey, you should never allow the "urgent and not important" to take over the "non-urgent and important" issues facing you.[15] Even so, you may fail to begin your succession plan because you feel you can't dedicate the time necessary to the planning process. You fear the rest of your business will suffer. You might ask yourself, "Why should I invest my important time on a matter that will only occur later when there are more pressing issues facing me right now?" Unfortunately, the longer you wait, the fewer options you will have.

You must recognize that succession planning is one of the great business practices to ensure the longevity of your business and maintain its value. It is my faith in this core recognition that led me to develop a system that is both efficient and effective. The Succession Solution^{SM}, which requires merely four days a year for a few hours a day, proves that you can achieve a succession plan that yields powerful and lasting results.

6. Self-serving adviser. You can fail to plan when you believe an adviser is recommending an approach that benefits only them. Unfortunately, some advisers intend to lead you down a path that ends in buying their products, and when you feel you are not in control of the process, you will abruptly end it, even to your own detriment.

The Succession Solution℠ puts you in control of the planning process. You must be involved in the process to have full confidence in the plan; only then will you be willing to see it through. With you at the helm, flanked by an expert team, and a designated team leader, the decisions you make will benefit your business, your family, and yourself.

7. Small pool of potential successors. You want to keep the family involved in the business. However, by limiting the potential candidates to family members only, you can be faced with selecting from a much smaller pool of qualified candidates than may be good for the future success of your business.

If potential successors are not properly trained, prepared, and willing to take the helm, you may feel you cannot let go or cede control for fear the next generation is not ready. Further, when selecting from a pool of family candidates only, you fear the possibility of alienating the candidates not selected.

Consequently, when you limit your successor to a family member, you create two forces you might have to overcome. First, you have limited your pool of potential candidates. Second, you have to pick among family members, which can create conflict. Famed investor Warren Buffet once compared family succession to "choosing the 2020 Olympic team by picking the eldest son of the gold-medal winner in the 2000 Olympics."[16]

When you use a defined process, however, and include other important stakeholders in the ongoing dynamic of succession planning, you can make better selections and manage the selection process. By starting early, you can often determine the skills required for next generation successors to assume the leadership role. Moreover, when you can show that the successor was selected on merit, your decision will be better supported by those impacted.

8. A single event. A common mistake is thinking the succession planning process is a single event. You might think that merely creating an estate plan—where a will, power of attorney, and living will are executed—is equal to creating a succession plan. It is not. Likewise, merely selecting a successor to become the next CEO does not complete your succession plan.

A succession plan is not a single event, but a process. It needs to be more holistic by considering the thoughts and ideas of as many impacted stakeholders as possible. Failure to consider how a succession plan will affect key stakeholders increases the likelihood that others will not accept—or worse, try to sabotage—your plan.

9. Cultural differences. Another challenge with succession planning can involve two opposing cultural forces. On the one hand, your family business may be grounded in generational history. For instance, your family may have built its company based on the actions and specific history of its founders and you may want to maintain that approach. On the other hand lies a very real opposing force—the need for all business and its owners to be focused on the future needs of the market and their personal lives. How your family business manages the productive tension of this dynamic will often impact the full attainment of your succession plan. When discussing the tensions between generations, it is often comically described as it being the job of the older generation to frustrate the younger generation and the job of the younger generation to irritate the older generation.

Let me share an example. I have a client, who over a period of forty years, created a successful real estate development company. The founder told me he would often work seven days a week building his company. He was careful with every dollar he spent in order to meet payroll. By the time he was ready to transfer his business to his two sons the real estate development company had more value and income than anyone would have imagined. The two sons were extremely competent and respectful of what their father had accomplished. Working with the family, we were able to successfully transfer the entire development company to the two sons.

After the transfer of the business, even though the father was financially secure, the father continued to work in the business. The sons appreciated the father's assistance and insight. However, not long after the transfer of the business, the father become irritated at the work ethic the two sons adopted. The father complained to the two sons and to me. The father did not understand why the sons did not work harder in the business and was concerned over the expensive lifestyles of his two sons. Having known the sons and how hard they actually worked, I explained to the father the sons were doing a great job and that he should be proud of them. Since the sons were so respectful of the father, neither son wanted to challenge their father.

Even though the sons grew the value of the business, the father continued to complain and grow frustrated with his sons. Eventually, one of the sons told his father he was tired of hearing from the father about the perceived lack of work ethic. The son told the father the reason the son did not work more in the business was based on the fact that his family was more important than the business. The father did not receive this message very well.

In my opinion, neither the son nor the father were wrong to have their views. Each one had different views and beliefs based on their life experiences. This is an example of a cultural difference. The important lesson is that you don't try to change someone's value system but rather communicate how best to proceed with the differences.

Fortunately, since the family had a good relationship with one another, they agreed to discuss the difficult issues. After a few meetings with the sons, both groups better understood the reasons for their different views. Because the father loved his sons and his grandchildren, the father accepted the sons' views. The sons also invited the father to more family events to show the father the value of their families. I am happy to report the business and the families are prospering even though the father still sometimes complains to me that he thinks his sons could work a bit harder.

10. Fearing conflict. As the saying goes, "Anticipation is often worse than reality." Only when you realize that conflict is a natural part of every relationship can you make genuine progress. The key is not to avoid or fear conflict, but to determine how you will deal with conflict when it arises. The Succession Solution^{SM} is designed to help you deal with conflict, and it contains various components specifically intended to address, discuss, and resolve troubling issues—without creating thermonuclear war within your family!

Keys to Chapter

1. With almost every succession plan, you will face challenges and detours. You need to embrace those challenges rather than ignore them.

2. You will have your own unique challenges. It is how you choose to address those challenges that will determine the success of your business transition.

3. The more you can identify roadblocks and detours at the start of the process, the more likely you will find solutions.

CHAPTER FIVE: THE FOUR COLLECTIVE COMMUNITIES TO ACKNOWLEDGE IN A SUCCESSION PLAN

"No man is above the law and no man is below it: nor do we ask any man's permission when we ask him to obey it."

– Theodore Roosevelt

A community can be defined as "a group of people with a common characteristic or interest living together within a larger society."[17] Communities operate best when its citizens or members understand the rules and responsibilities within the community. When citizens know the rules and regulations of their community, there is greater certainty among its citizens. With greater certainty comes efficiency and productivity. Similarly, penalties for violating the laws of the community need to be clear, so each citizen understands the consequences of both good and bad behavior. A closely held business is a community. Within that community, there are a number of interdependent, separate communities.

It is important that you set forth rules for the communities within your business. While you may not need a set of regulations like the Internal Revenue Service has punished us with, it is important to set forth basic rules, standards, and expectations for your company. By setting forth rules that are important to you and your company, everyone who interacts with your company will have better clarity of their responsibility, or if they want to work with your company at all.

The guidelines of your business will emanate from your core principles and values. Policies that align with your principles will provide clarity to everyone in your company. Further, when a conflict arises, you can look to your values to address the dispute. This is why one of the very first steps in The Succession Solution℠ is to develop your core values and vision. By defining your core values, you will be better equipped to determine if the rules and responsibilities of your company derive from those values.

Within almost every closely held business, there are four separate but interdependent communities that operate. The four communities are: (i) those who own the company, (ii) those who govern the company, (iii) those who lead the company, and (iv) those who are employed by the company. When developing your succession plan, review each of these communities to ensure you develop a set of rules for each community to follow. If you find that certain policies are in conflict with your fundamental values and vision for your company, then amend the rules to be in alignment with your core principles. Otherwise, when a conflict between your guidelines and your principles exists, you will have a difficult time resolving the dispute.

I. Ownership

The first community within your company is comprised of the owners. There are a variety of forms in which ownership can occur or operate. You can operate as a corporation, limited liability company (LLC), or a partnership. Regardless of the form of entity, the owners need a set of rules to follow and understand. For the purposes of this chapter, I will use the term "company" for all three entities.

Basic Rights of Ownership

With any company, ownership grants you three distinct and basic rights: (i) the right to choose who will govern your company (board of directors), (ii) the right to receive dividends, and (iii) the right to proceeds if your company is liquidated. However, you can amend, expand, restrict, or eliminate some of the three basic rights when developing your succession plan.

Consider the following when developing your ownership succession strategy:

a. Who can own equity in the company? Will it be restricted to all family members, or only family members who work in the business? Or will you allow others to own equity in the business?

b. Do you want to have different rights of ownership? For instance, you can choose to have voting and non-voting ownership. Non-voting owners will enjoy dividends and liquidations but will not have a right to elect board members.

c. What rights do you want to provide to existing shareholders? Will they have the right to transfer their equity to a family member, child, or a trust for the benefit of a child or spouse?

d. Will there be situations where an owner will be required to sell his stock? For instance, do you want to buy the equity upon the owner's death, termination from employment, or in the event a creditor sues the owner for the stock?

e. How will the value of an owner's equity be determined? An owner who is forced to sell his stock due to a death or termination of employment may want to know how his ownership will be valued. This will also be important for the company to know in order to determine its liquidity requirements upon a repurchase of equity. This is often one of the most difficult matters to resolve. Your CPA should be able to provide guidance and options for you to consider.

f. If there will be a purchase of an owner's equity, will there be a period of time during which the company or other owners can purchase the equity? In order to avoid a financial strain on the company, the owners of a company will often agree on a period of time to purchase the equity.

g. Often, a company or other shareholders will purchase life insurance on one another in order to fund the purchase of stock in the event of a shareholder's death. If the shareholders are insurable, this provides liquidity for the company, and it can provide security for the deceased owners's family.

h. Will the company be forced to make certain minimum distributions or dividends each year? Owners of specific types of companies (LLCs and S corporations) are personally taxed on the net income of the company. Consequently, if the company does not make a distribution to its owners, the owners will be required to pay taxes from their own savings. Often with these types of companies, the owners will require the company to make minimum distributions to pay the taxes attributable to the company's profits.

When developing your succession plan, begin with deciding how your ownership group will handle the three rights of ownership. Since the owners of the company ultimately decide how the company will be governed, you can't make much progress if you don't reach a consensus among the owners.

Of course, a company can operate without a consensus among its owners. However, unless there is an owner who controls a majority of the ownership, deadlocks can occur. Further, if there is a loss of control among an ownership group (due to a death, divorce, or some other unforeseen event), your company will then be directed by the next group of majority owners. Your company can continue to operate in this situation, but there will be much less certainty for each one of the four communities in your company. Lack of uncertainly is dangerous, because it breeds confusion, lack of trust, and potential failure in succession.

II. Governance

The second community within your company that you will examine as part of your succession plan will be those who will govern the business of the company. This will be the board of directors within a corporation, the board of managers within an LLC, and the general partners within a limited partnership. Again, for the purposes of this section, I will refer to "the board" for all three types of business.

Role of the Board

The board is generally responsible for fundamental decisions made on behalf of your company. The board is elected by the owners of your company who hold voting ownership rights. Non-voting owners, if your company has them, will not participate in the selection of your board.

The board acts in the best interest of your company and on behalf of you as the company's owner. If you are appointed to a board, you have a legal duty to all shareholders. You must be careful not to make decisions which would benefit you to the detriment of your company. In fact, if you find yourself in a situation where you would be conflicted in your decision making, you should abstain from the decision-making process. An example of a conflict of interest would be the CEO of a company sitting in on the board's decision about what to compensate the CEO.

The board will typically approve or set the long-term strategy for your company. The board will also hire the CEO or president of your company, and will be responsible for reviewing and setting the compensation and incentives for both roles. Other fundamental decisions made by the board include whether or not to sell your company, if your company should buy another company, and how your company will make distributions to its owners.

The board functions between the owners and the leaders who run your company on a daily basis. As a result, the selection of board members and rules under which you design your board is critical. A well-functioning board will periodically communicate to its owners the condition of the company, including reporting on the financial condition, strategy, and concerns of the company. A good board will also seek input from the owners of the company.

When there is only one owner of a company, there is little difference between the owner and the governance of the company. The sole owner often acts in the role of board member and CEO. It is when there is more than one owner of a company that governance becomes more important.

When there is more than one owner of a company, the owners need to decide who will be on the board and how decisions will be made. For instance, when one owner or group of owners owns a majority of the equity of a company, that owner or group of owners will often control the board and the direction of the company. This can be an extremely powerful position for a majority owner, especially in a family business. Majority owners who control the board can set the compensation of the officers or decide whether to issue dividends.

This talk of majority control reminds me of a second-generation business I knew of whose founder was struggling to decide how best to transfer his stock to his two sons. The younger of the two sons was a friend of mine, and he was just entering the family business. My friend's father was trying to decide whether to give his oldest son majority ownership of the company. When my friend balked, his father asked him if he knew the value of minority interest in a very successful business. My very astute but respectful friend answered by stating that the value of the minority interest would be what the majority owner decided it would be. Fortunately for my friend, his father realized the wisdom in his son's answer and made the two brothers equal owners. Since that time, the two siblings have successfully grown the business and are now working on their succession plan.

As ownership becomes more extended, it is important to decide who will be on the board, and how certain board decisions should be made. I have seen some scenarios where various family groups agree that each branch of the family will select one board member to represent the group. In other situations, various owners will agree to place their ownership in a trust and appoint trustees who will appoint the board members.

Whatever succession plan you develop, ensure that the governance follows the values and goals of your plan. In fact, one of the fundamental roles of the board should be the implementation of your company's succession plan.

Listed here are several other matters you will want to consider when developing the governance structure for the implementation of your succession plan:

a. How many times will the board meet?

b. Will each group of owners be represented on the board?

c. Will you require a certain number of independent board members?

d. How will you compensate the board?

e. How many members do you want on the board?

f. Will your company provide director's and officer's liability insurance?

g. What type of training will you provide for each member of the board?

h. What qualification(s) will be required to be a board member?

i. What will be the criteria for the board in selecting a CEO or president?

There may also be certain fundamental decisions that require a super-majority of the board to decide. Owners of family-operated businesses often feel strongly about a certain industry they want or don't want to operate in. You may also require a super majority for the selection of the CEO, the sale of a large division, or the sale of the entire company.

Be cautious when considering whether to adopt an issue that will require a super majority or a unanimous vote. In these situations, you effectively increase the power of the minority owners of your company. When you agree to adopt certain super majority decisions, you are effectively giving the minority owners more control in your company with respect to any supermajority vote that is required.

Fortunately, there are a great deal of resources available to you when deciding on how best to set up the governance of your company in order to implement your succession plan. An experienced business attorney or consultant can often provide you with various options to consider.

As noted above, an important governance decision is whether or not you want to have independent board members. An independent board member is someone who is not an owner of the company, employee, or a relation of either an employee or owner.

It is considered best practice to have a number of independent board members. An independent board member is able to provide objective feedback without the fear or concern of family or employee retribution. The independent member is less emotionally invested in the issue. In an article in the *McKinsey Quarterly*, it was reported that companies that have survived three generations tend to have strong boards that usually included a significant number of outside directors.[18]

Independent board members can be very helpful in a family business. An independent board member can challenge other members when family issues are raised and a family board member becomes too emotionally invested in the issue to make the right decision for your company.

Another value of an independent board member involves CEO evaluation and compensation. When the CEO is a family member, it is hard for other family board members to make a decision about CEO compensation without either the CEO or the family board members feeling they have been unfairly treated. An independent board member or members, on the other hand, can be part of the compensation committee for the CEO. This can create more accountability for the CEO, because independent board members will not fear punishment from him/her when they set reasonable goals and objectives for the CEO. Similarly, other family board members should not feel the CEO is over-compensated because the independent compensation committee set the compensation in a reasonable manner.

III. Leadership

The third community within your company is comprised of the officers, otherwise referred to as the executive group or team. The executive team typically consists of the chief executive officer/president (CEO), chief operating officer (COO), and the chief financial officer (CFO). The board will hire the CEO. Afterwards, the CEO will typically hire the COO or CFO. However, due to the vital role of the CEO within your company and his potential interactions with the board, the board should be involved in reviewing the CEO's selection of his team. For the purposes of this book, I will refer to both the CEO and the president as the CEO.

While the board legally hires and approves all the officers of your company, it ought to consider a process for the selection of the CEO in particular, and what qualifications he must possess. By establishing a process and qualifications, the board can often eliminate future complications. The appropriate process can, for example, prevent the installment of a family member who thinks he ought to be the CEO, even though he doesn't possess the appropriate level of experience, education, or other necessary qualifications to run your company. By establishing criteria beforehand, you can make an otherwise difficult situation a bit easier.

I have worked with clients who believe, due to the nature of their business, that a family member must be the CEO. Conversely, I have seen where family business owners refuse to allow a family member to act as the CEO. In both situations, the decision was the correct one, and everyone was comfortable with the plan. Whatever you decide, make it clear to the board and owners so you can avoid any future conflicts.

To be fair, and to avoid a potential conflict between the CEO and the board, the board should establish the responsibilities for the CEO, as well as a review process to evaluate and provide feedback to the CEO. The CEO should also be told how he or she will be compensated in the most objective manner possible.

Because there are no bright lines of demarcation, one topic you may wish to consider when developing your succession plan is the involvement of the board with your company. I have seen too many cases where board members want to meddle in the affairs of the CEO. This is dangerous, because often the board member does not have the qualifications or the knowledge of the company like the CEO. There is a common saying when addressing this issue: "Nose in fingers out." The saying refers to the distinction between a board's obligation to stick its nose in a company's governance matters, but to keep its fingers out of the management of the company.

If you do decide to have a family member as the CEO, in addition to having objective criteria for the evaluation and compensation of your CEO, consider establishing a compensation committee made up of certain members of the board. It will be the compensation committee's job to establish guidelines, conduct reviews, and make recommendations to the full board.

This is where independent board members become invaluable. If you decide to appoint independent board members to the board, having them serve on the compensation committee is another good way to avoid the perception of either over compensation by other family members or under compensation by the CEO. The decisions of the compensation committee are free from challenges rooted in family rivalry, especially if the committee is made up of independent board members.

IV. Employment

The fourth community within your company is the employees. The employees are hired by the officers or executive team of your company. Since an employee's responsibility is to carry out the requests of your company's executive team, employees are not supposed to be hired by owners of your company or members of the board. When an employee is hired without the consent and approval of the officers of your company, problems can arise by creating conflict between the new employee and the officers. It can also send a bad message to the rest of your employees.

Whether your company is family owned or not, establishing employment practices as part of your succession plan can avoid a potential conflict at a later date. I have seen many situations where multiple owners of a company have a great working relationship among themselves, but they want nothing to do with spouses. Trying to fire, compensate, or evaluate the spouse of a fellow owner can be fraught with conflict. The owner married to the employed spouse is stuck between siding with his/her spouse or his/her fellow owner. How do you think that will end?

You can often avoid these types of situations by simply establishing a hiring policy ahead of time.

Some owners of family businesses, however, want and may even encourage family members to join the business. In fact, a family business can actually have a bonding effect on families by bringing them together in working toward a common goal. When family members work and struggle together, it can bring them closer than they were before.

If you decide to allow a family member to work in the company, then you should set up certain criteria for employment. For example, some companies require an heir to work three to five years elsewhere before they can be employed by the company. Establishing this type of requirement is effective, because the potential employee will have learned employment practices in a non-family situation.

You may also want to consider whether or not you want to employ in-laws in your company. I encountered a situation where an in-law was employed by a family business and subsequently divorced from the majority owner's daughter. The situation became difficult because the employee was performing at such a high level that the owner did not want to let him go. However, the owner was under great pressure at home from his wife to fire the employee. The employee eventually left, but it created significant anxiety for everyone in the organization.

The board or the executive team of your business can establish these rules for employment. By allowing either one of these two groups to establish guidelines, you show your organization—as well as your family—that your company should be run like a business.

If you follow your company's values and principles in establishing the policies and guidelines for these four communities, you will demonstrate to everyone in your company your expectations for the operation of your company. Further, by establishing clear, understandable, and fair guidelines, your company will be better prepared to handle the situation when a conflict does arise.

Keys to the Chapter

1. There are four fundamental communities within a company: (i) ownership, (ii) governance, (iii) leadership, and (iv) employment.

2. Like any other community, each community within your company needs policies and procedures to operate better.

3. The rules and policies of your company should be grounded in your company's values and principles.

4. Setting rules and regulations now will enable you to better manage a conflict later.

CHAPTER SIX: PRACTICAL ISSUES TO CONSIDER WITH SUCCESSION PLANNING

"Wisdom consists of the anticipation of consequences."

– Norman Cousins

Cornelius Vanderbilt's railroad empire earned him a fortune consistently ranked among the top three in American history. In 2013 dollars, his net worth at the time of his death in 1877 would be a staggering $205 billion.[19] When the industrialist died, he left almost his entire estate to his son William. Cornelius left nothing to his other sons because he believed only William capable of maintaining the Vanderbilt business, and, boy was he right! By the time William died in 1885, only nine years after his father, he had doubled the value of the business empire and was the wealthiest man in the United States. Even though Cornelius's decision may have alienated his other family members, the core of his succession plan involved selecting the best person to take over the business.

William's succession plan, on the other hand, was not so savvy. Instead of selecting one family member to follow him in managing the business and maintaining the family's vast holdings and wealth, William chose to divide his estate among his eight children. Maybe he felt he needed to divide the business to be "fair."

Unfortunately, due to lavish spending by the third and fourth generations of Vanderbilts, followed by the Great Depression and the institution of income and estate taxes, the family fortune practically vanished within thirty years of William's death.

Do you think William anticipated the consequences of his succession plan? Do you think he prepared the next generation to handle such wealth? Was William willing or able to make these difficult decisions?

Of course, it is possible that he just didn't care about what happened, but I have a hard time believing that someone entrusted with so much affluence would take such an attitude of complacency.

Vanderbilt's story serves as a crucial example of what can happen when succession planning is ignored. If a lack of future planning could evaporate one of the largest fortunes America has ever seen, just imagine what a similar oversight could do to yours. Before proceeding with your succession plan, consider the risks inherent in your choices. Disregarding your own succession planning process can result in potentially devastating consequences. As William Vanderbilt's story demonstrates, a succession planning process is essential.

Although you should consider the potential consequences of succession planning, do not allow your concerns to prevent you from taking action. In fact, allow them to do the exact opposite. By keeping potential consequences clearly in mind, you can weigh those consequences against positive outcomes before deciding if and how you want to proceed. When you consider the outcomes of succession planning, you may discover that those consequences you initially perceived as negative are not so bad at all.

In short, confronting the potential outcomes of your own succession plan is an extremely valuable exercise. Once you list and discuss any perceived negative aspects to succession planning, you will realize these factors are not as challenging as they once seemed. More often than not, it is fear of the unknown or lack of knowledge that can stop a succession plan in its tracks.

To use a medical analogy, when most people meet with a doctor to discuss undergoing an operation or taking a certain medication, they want to know the risks associated with the operation or the side effects of the medication. Once they have been informed of any adverse effects, they are better prepared to make a decision.

Similarly, as part of your succession planning analysis, compare and contrast the potential benefits and detriments you and your company may experience. For instance, if you recognize that the family member to whom you had planned to transfer the business is in fact ill-prepared for the job, you may decide not to proceed. Instead, you might hire someone else, opt to sell the company, or have it dissolved at your passing.

To be clear, though, even deciding not to plan is a plan. As my mother so often told me, "Deciding not to take action on a matter is still making a decision."

Practical Planning Considerations

1. You need to take care of number one. A common problem when embarking on a succession plan is focusing too much on your business or family and forgetting about yourself. I have seen founders and/or spouses who are so concerned with providing for their business and children that they don't plan for their own financial security.

If you decide to transfer management, ownership, or control to the next generation, you must first understand your own financial needs, especially if some form of the income you had relied upon will no longer be available. Meet with your financial adviser to evaluate your fiscal situation prior to any succession planning. Do you have enough assets for you and your spouse to live comfortably for the remainder of your lives? Do you rely on income from the business to support your lifestyle? It is crucial that you answer these questions as you consider your succession plan.

2. You need to reach an agreement on price. With practically any succession plan, you and your team must determine and agree upon the value of your business. Determining the value can be challenging in any negotiation, but it can become far more difficult when your family members are involved. Nonetheless, an evaluation of your business is critical in determining the purchase price to be paid by the next generation. Even if you choose to give your ownership away, an estimation of your business's worth will still be necessary.

The IRS requires taxpayers to file a federal gift tax return for any gifts in excess of a certain dollar amount ($15,000 for 2019). Filing a federal gift tax return for a closely-held business entails declaring the gift's value, and this value should be determined by a valuation expert and included with the gift tax return. Because the specific method or technique used to value your business can produce a wide range of prices, deciding on how your team will arrive on a purchase price can be challenging.

3. You change from CEO/entrepreneur to banker. Often, when the transfer of your business occurs, you will sell a portion of the business to the next generation. Because it is difficult to obtain commercial financing from a bank to support such a sale, you or your company may elect to self-finance the loan. When this situation occurs, your role changes from CEO to lender, and it must be recognized that this sale will represent a large part of your retirement or estate at your passing.

In this situation, new questions arise. What type of security will you demand? With a traditional lender such as a bank, security for payment would likely be required, including personal guarantees from the borrower and the borrower's spouse. Additionally, a bank would likely restrict the amount of money the borrower could take out of the company. When you become the banker, you must prepare yourself in the event of a default. Are you willing to sue your children and their spouses for payment? Would you be willing to exercise your rights under your loan documents to take back the stock in payment for the company? These can be very difficult questions to answer if your business experiences a financial challenge. However, you must anticipate the consequences of non-payment if you are considering selling your ownership interests to the next generation.

4. You need to understand the role of your advisers. Part of any strong succession plan involves selecting a team of capable advisers. While you may be able to produce a plan on your own, you'll be stronger and more effective with a talented team. Not only will your advisory team help you plan and avoid unforeseen landmines, they can also offer unanticipated strategies for reaching your goal successfully. Provided each professional has the necessary skill set, your team will typically consist of your CPA, a financial adviser, a succession planning consultant, and a lawyer.

Keep in mind that issues and/or conflicts can arise in determining and understanding who exactly these advisers represent. Do they act for you, the company, or the other stakeholders? If one group thinks they are not being properly spoken for, they may not respect the advice of the advisers, who may then be perceived as representing your interests only. Thus, it is important from the outset that your advisers be transparent about their advocacy to ensure that everyone is comfortable with the team.

Another concern in the selection of advisers is competence—both in their field and in the succession planning process. You would not go to your cardiologist to repair a broken arm, no matter how wonderful that cardiologist may be. It's imperative that your advisers be specialists in succession planning.

You also need to consider how you want to bring your team of advisers together. You may have selected a great group of advisers, but if they don't understand your objectives, as well as their individual roles, conflict and confusion can occur among the advisers. Schedule a meeting with your advisers early on so you can discuss your expectations and determine how and where each adviser can assist in the process. This will help avoid duplication of efforts and allow better communications with your team.

5. Once you start, don't stop. If there is one thing you'll want to consider before starting the succession planning process, it's this: What will happen if you start the process and then later decide to stop? Of course, up until you agree on a process and begin to execute a plan, you can stop or change your mind at any time. But initiating a process only to interrupt it mid-stream can create significant ill-will, a loss of regard for the process itself, and possibly even a loss of respect for you.

Almost every succession plan requires that important matters be addressed and sensitive issues be managed. What's more, when a process is begun and then stopped, the stumbling-block issue typically gets worse. Stopping the process mid-stream can be perceived as a refusal to let go, and this can undermine relationships. It can also create significant uncertainty and anxiety with your stakeholders. Key personnel can be lost when succession planning is interrupted, and employees do not understand why. People can't help but fear for their own futures.

I worked with a client who began a succession planning process with all the intent and desire to find a successor CEO within the family. The client engaged a renowned adviser to test and score the potential candidates. The adviser interviewed all the candidates along with the rest of top management, then prepared and delivered a detailed report on each candidate. However, fearing the impact the findings would have on the family, the client did not follow the recommendations. What ensued over the following years was more intra-family discord and rivalry. Top management became concerned and anxious whether ownership could make the difficult family decision for the benefit of the company.

Years later, I was engaged to resurrect the process. One of the first and most difficult issues I had to address was why they wanted to go through succession planning if they were not going to respect the process. Fortunately, I convinced the group by showing them the steps I intended to follow in order to not only develop a plan, but also to implement the plan. Only after the group felt confident the process would be respected did we successfully develop a succession plan to follow.

I have found that most often, action will produce far greater results than inaction. Mark Twain once said, "Twenty years from now you will be more disappointed by the things you didn't do than by the ones you did do."

6. You will upset, alienate, or anger someone involved in the process. As the poet John Lydgate stated (a quote often attributed to Abraham Lincoln), "You can please some of the people all of the time, you can please all of the people some of the time, but you can't please all of the people all of the time." Lydgate could have been a succession planning adviser!

When you understand this perspective and encourage everyone to adopt it, the process will move more smoothly. Consensus on every significant step in a succession planning process is a rare occurrence. You will need to break at least a few eggs to make your succession plan omelet.

Before you undertake any succession planning process, you and other important stakeholders should agree that no plan will ever be perfect. Any plan you develop can be modified and improved upon when and if you discover it needs adjusting. In the end, the success of the overall plan should take primacy over the needs of a particular stakeholder.

It is important to note that the desire to keep the peace is one of the most common reasons succession plans don't progress. You just don't want the aggravation of trying to please everyone around the table, and you may fear the loss of a valuable relationship. These hesitations are completely understandable. Few will argue that their business is more important than their family or a family relationship. Thus, if you are facing this situation, you must determine if you can navigate a process that allows maintaining family relationships as well as transferring the business on to another.

7. Your customers may leave. Perhaps you enjoy a very special relationship with your clients, and you fear—sometimes rightfully so—that the client may leave and go to a competitor once you're no longer working in the business. This can be a real or perceived concern.

To illustrate, I recently met with my financial adviser of over twenty years. There are few professional relationships closer than the one with your personal financial adviser. At our meeting, my adviser introduced me to his son and shared that he, along with other family members, would soon be taking over my business. I must admit, I was initially taken back. When I got home and told my wife about the situation, however, she said without hesitation, "This is great. Now we will have someone to look to when our original adviser retires." I wondered if I had been a bit shortsighted.

Conversely, a close relationship with a client can also work against you. I have another client who told me his most significant customer was concerned about whether or not he had developed a succession plan. The customer was worried about the smooth supply of goods during a transition and was afraid that if something happened to the client, the supply of goods could stop. Clearly, an abrupt halt of goods would negatively impact the customer's own business, so he wanted to know who was going to replace the client in the event of a business conversion. As a result of this conversation, during the succession planning process, we made sure that this key customer was able to meet and approve of the successor.

8. Your banker objects or you remain personally liable. Almost every business owner I have worked with has some type of obligation with a lender. In some of these situations, the company may be the official borrower, but the business owner may still be personally liable to the bank in the event of a company default. If you decide to transfer your business to a new generation of owners, you may want to speak to your banker. The loan officer may have full confidence in your ability to run the company but may object to your proposed successor.

Further, if you are personally liable to a bank for your business's debt, you must consider how you'll address this liability as you contemplate the transfer of your business. Extracting yourself from a personal guarantee to a banker is extremely hard. I have one client, for instance, who has done a great job with his succession plan. He has transferred the operations and some of the equity to his very able sons, yet he has not yet transferred control of the business. The sole reason for his decision is that the bank will not release him from his personal guarantee, and the client does not feel comfortable transferring the business to his sons until he is released by the bank.

9. You select the wrong person. In any succession planning process, there is a valid risk of selecting the wrong person for your replacement. Particularly in a family situation, the possibility of a wrong selection is increased due to a smaller pool of candidates. In many family-owned business situations, there is a shared desire to pick among the next generation of family members for a successor. There is nothing wrong with this approach, but it must be acknowledged that when your family decides to limit the pool of successor owners or managers, you limit your decision, and this may increase the risk of making the wrong choice.

Selecting a successor is vital to the succession planning process. If you don't select one when you are able, then a successor will emerge by default. Ask yourself: Are you and your business better positioned with a successor selected by default, or one chosen after a thoughtful process of discovery, training, and experience?

10. Your successor is not ready when you are. Even if you develop the best succession plan possible, there is an essential second part to the process: the execution of that plan. The implementation of your succession plan must be performed as carefully as was the development of the plan itself. Consequently, deciding to select your daughter to be the next CEO or majority owner is only a first step; you then need to make sure she is ready for the role.

Leadership training for the next generation is among a president or CEO's most important roles. To use an analogy, imagine your next leader as the graduating star quarterback of his college. Most NFL coaches don't put their rookie quarterback into the first game, no matter how wonderful their college career may have been. The young NFL prospect needs additional training for this new and more challenging position. Ask Hall of Fame quarterback John Elway about his rookie season when he faced the Pittsburgh Steelers defense.[20] It was not a good day for Elway, but he got a whole lot better with training.

Like a successful coach, your job is to groom your star successor for the job. Rather than expecting he or she will be able to step in and start right away, remember that as with the rookie quarterback, the more reps and training your successor experiences, the better prepared he or she will be to assume this key new role. What's more, accepting that some setbacks will likely occur will make it easier on everyone involved.

11. You think retiring as CEO means losing control. Believing that retiring as CEO equates to loss of control may be one of the biggest misconceptions you can make about succession planning. You might fear that initiating the succession planning process leads to a single destination—loss of control or ownership.

A few years ago, I worked with an elderly CEO who had majority control of the stock in his company. When his children were much younger, he had transferred some of his stock equally among them. However, only one of his children worked in the business, and only he wanted to assume the role as CEO and operate the company after the passing of his father. The business owner shared with me that although he would like to transfer more ownership to this son, he couldn't, because he would lose control. I asked him if he would be interested in learning how he could transfer more stock to his son without losing voting control, and his curt response was that it could not be done. I then explained the concept of issuing his son non-voting stock. By the time we were done, we had transferred ownership of practically all of the father's stock to the son—everything except for the voting control.

This is just one of many examples of how management, and even ownership, can be transferred without necessarily giving up control.

12. You can't be fair and equal. Equal does not necessarily mean the same thing as fair. Equal is a numerical calculation while fair requires the consideration of many more factors than mere math. Once your succession plan is complete, it may appear that you are treating one child more numerically favorably than another, and this may be the case. This does not mean your plan is not fair or correct. Depending on how you and your team view the plan, you may decide that you need to leave your business to those family members who are working in it. I have worked with many family-business owners who believe it is vital that a company owner play an active working role within the company. In such a case, there may not be enough assets to divide equally so everyone gets an equivalent value.

Obviously, deciding what is fair is dependent upon how you determine value or what is fair. What is the value of a closely-held business's stock when you have a minority interest? In most cases, a minority interest means you can't force the company to issue you a bonus, buy your stock, or do much of anything without the vote of the majority. Is it fair to give a family member a minority interest in an attempt to equalize the division of your wealth?

I have also witnessed more than one situation in which one family member was given the stock in a company, while the rest of the family inherited the remainder of the estate. Unfortunately, the family member who had received the stock ended up with nothing after the company went out of business.

When working through your succession plan, understand that being fair and equal to all family members may not be possible. You must be willing to explore both potential and perceived negative consequences and do the best you can in any given context.

Keys to Chapter

1. While it is important to consider all the stakeholders affected by a succession process, don't forget that you are among the most important of those stakeholders.

2. Most often, action will produce far greater results than inaction. Mark Twain once said, "Twenty years from now you will be more disappointed by the things you didn't do than by the ones you did do."

3. Remember, you don't have to give up control to transfer ownership.

4. Understand how your role can change when you implement your plan, and how that new role may create different issues that you will need to consider.

CHAPTER SEVEN: FAIR MAY BE EQUAL, BUT EQUAL MAY NOT BE FAIR

"I'm your older brother, Mike, and I was stepped over!"

"That's the way Pop wanted it."

"It ain't the way I wanted it! I can handle things! I'm smart! Not like everybody says... like dumb... I'm smart and I want respect!"

–Fredo & Michael Corleone, The Godfather: Part II

For centuries, scholars, business owners, and society have debated about how we can decide what is fair and how we can develop a fair process. After all, how can we possibly consider all the factors involved in being fair? What factors should we ignore or prioritize? Do we look to the past to determine who should be rewarded in the future? What happens if our outcome is different than what we had anticipated? Do we try to modify something else to address the unintended result?

Let me illustrate with a simple example. Imagine a mother has one candy bar but two children, Kate and Alex, who both want it. The mother decides a fair process would be to flip a coin. Since each child has an equal chance of getting that candy bar, the mother can't be criticized for any favoritism. However, when Kate wins the candy bar and Alex does not, Alex will almost certainly argue the process was not fair.

The next day, the mother has another candy bar. Should she maintain the same coin-flipping process so each child has an equal chance of winning? Or should she change the process to equalize what had happened the day before? However, if the mother decides to change the process and give today's candy bar to Alex, Kate may argue that changing the process at this time is unfair.

Would it have been fairer if the mother had merely split the candy bar in half and given half to Kate and half to Alex? What if Alex had just returned from a friend's house and been given the exact same candy bar a few hours earlier? Or what if one child had done something to merit a candy bar while the other had spent the day misbehaving?

These simple examples demonstrate that determining what is fair is not as easy as one might initially think. As a business owner, you will also need to consider how or if you will want to address the thorny area of "fairness" when it comes to your business's transition process.

I've heard many clients tell me they want to be "fair" to the next generation. In the same conversation, they will tell me that, in order to be fair, they want to treat everyone equally. In other words, they believe that by treating everyone equally, they are inherently treating them fairly.

In fact, a 2018 Business Owners' Perspective study by MassMutual found that 60% of business owners want to split their assets *equally* among their families. Beyond this, for 64% of business owners, the business is the largest asset they have . From these statistics, it appears that, unless there is only one child in the family, multiple children will own the business interests of the senior generation.

While the decision to transfer ownership in a business is ultimately the owner's decision, it is important to recognize the differences between fair and equal. After all, how the business owner decides to transfer his or her business interest and how the transfer is viewed by the next generation can materially impact the likelihood of a business's successful succession.

To add to this challenge, many business owners find that the next generation of family members often each have their own definitions for what is "fair." These various family members may not believe that dividing assets equally means that they are being treated fairly, or that their parents are acting fairly. For example, think of a next-generation family member who decides to come into the family business and sacrifices his or her other dreams for the sake of the family business. Later, the parents tell this family member that they want to be fair to all their children and think the business should be divided equally among all the siblings. Do you think the child who has contributed years of service will think he or she has been treated fairly?

Is Equal Fair?

From a definitional perspective, the term "equal" is a numerical calculation. Things are equal if they are of the same quantity, size, degree, or value. With respect to the division of assets, equal would then simply mean that you take the total value of the assets, and divide it among the group you identify as your beneficiaries (whether that group consists of family members or employees).

However, it's certainly not that simple in a business. For instance, the value of assets is seldom fixed and determinable. Almost every asset you own will either increase or decrease in value over time. Another thing to consider is that how and when you decide to determine the value of a business can also produce different results. Some assets will be more liquid than others. Some assets will have more tax and carrying costs associated with them. For example, would you rather receive an Individual Retirement Account (IRA) valued at $1,000,000, or an apartment building valued at $1,000,000? You might prefer the real estate due to the fact that, if you were a beneficiary of the IRA, you'd be required to withdraw the IRA over a ten-year period and report the entire amount as taxable income. However, the real estate can be held for years without recognizing any income. Conversely, depending on the location of the real estate, you might prefer to own the IRA because you want the liquidity associated with it.

Many years ago, an elderly client asked if I would act as the executor of his estate when he passed away. The client had three adult sons who did not get along and whom the client did not trust to handle his estate.

The client wanted to divide his assets equally among his three sons. Besides a number of other assets, the client owned several residential apartment buildings. While I felt it was a compliment to be asked by my client to act as his executor, at the time, I did not realize what I was getting myself into.

When the client passed away, I discovered the rental properties were in severe disrepair, under-insured, and potential fire hazards. As the executor, I was personally liable to secure the assets of the estate. I was incredibly nervous that an accident might occur on the property. Frankly, I suppose this is a perfect example of the old saying, "Be careful what you wish for."

The three sons knew about the status of the real estate, and none of them wanted the assets transferred to them. Rather, each one wanted the other assets in the estate transferred to them. As a result, I liquidated the rental property (at a discounted value) as quickly as possible due to the potential liability associated with it. This story illustrates quite clearly how difficult it can be to determine asset value when trying to divide assets equally.

To put it bluntly: trying to be fair is a difficult task when you own a closely-held business. Even if you agree that fair does not mean equal, then how can you still be fair? When determining the value of your business and how to distribute it fairly, how do you consider the contributions made by a family member who has worked in the business? I have heard many next-generation family members argue that they helped grow the business. However, in some of those same situations, the senior generation will respond, "so did a bunch of other folks, and you don't see them getting any ownership."

The good news is that while trying to be fair may be difficult, there are a number of steps you can follow to help. This chapter will explain these steps so you and other important stakeholders can develop a decision-making process that everyone believes has treated them fairly.

Creating a Fair Decision-Making Process in 5 Steps

When we make decisions on difficult business issues, the goal should be a result that does the following: (i) best serves the needs of the business (ii) aligns with the business's core principles or values, and (iii) does not harm anyone.

Next, you need to understand that decisions about what is fair can only be made with the available data. Accordingly, don't think you will ever have everything you need to make the decision. After all, business owners make business decisions every day with the available data. You should not delay the process worrying about what the IRS, Congress, or the next pandemic may bring. As the saying goes, *"you can't wait for all the lights to turn green before you start driving."*

Decisions about what is fair should also be made in an environment of honest and open dialogue, and with an attempt to remove bias. It is vital to understand and appreciate the real value of fairness is in the *process* of decision making, not in the outcome.

To set up a fair decision-making process for challenging issues, I recommend you follow the five steps below:

1. Include important stakeholders in the process while being as transparent as possible.

2. Have the group of stakeholders define and develop a decision-making process for the issue.

3. Explain how the decision-making process was determined to the people impacted by it.

4. Test the process against your core principles and values.

5. Consistently apply the process when needed.

Let's take the compensation of a family member as an example. Often, next-generation owners who are not involved in the business feel that the next-generation owners currently working in the business are overpaid or enjoy too many perquisites. On the other hand, the next generation working in the business may feel that they are underpaid or not recognized for their efforts. This can put senior-generation business owners in a difficult situation. The business owner wants to be fair to their employees, but also does not want to be viewed as unfair to the family members *not* involved in the business. This can get even more complicated if the next generation not involved in the business actually owns a portion of the company.

In this situation, I recommend the business owner begin by involving each important stakeholder. Since compensation can be a very personal issue, the business owner may not want to seek input as to *how much* someone should be paid. Rather, I would suggest that the business owner ask each stakeholder *how* the compensation should be determined.

Once the business owner seeks the input of each important stakeholder, everyone can meet to develop a process for determining compensation. Again, I would avoid deciding on amounts and instead focus on how compensation should be determined.

One effective process to deal with sensitive compensation issues would be to form a compensation committee. If you already have an active board of directors, this is a common subcommittee. As part of forming the compensation committee, you may agree to ensure that there are independent board members or advisers on it. This will take away some of the potential personal issues that can pop up when dealing with family members.

After the compensation process is decided, you would then tell those impacted by the process. Those impacted might include the key employee, other owners, employees, or in-laws of owners.

As part of the development of the process to decide compensation, one important thing to do is make sure it fits with your company's culture. Personally, I like to do this by looking at the core values of a company to make sure the process fits in with them. When the culture squares to your process, you can be more confident that you have chosen the right approach.

If you do decide to use your compensation committee to determine the compensation of your key stakeholders, then regardless of the actual compensation paid to the employee, the key stakeholders should not complain that the process of deciding the compensation was unfair.

The final step here is to ensure this decision-making process is followed on a consistent basis. When there is a departure from the process, there should be a very compelling reason for the departure. Otherwise, the likelihood of someone complaining that they have not been treated fairly is quite high.

Acknowledge the Different Lens of Fairness

Anytime you involve other important stakeholders in a process to determine what is fair, keep in mind that there will always be some individuals who interpret the situation differently, despite looking at the same situation with the same facts. Don't view this as something negative, but try to embrace it as part of the process.

Like beauty, fairness is in the eye of the beholder. Depending on who you ask, you may get different answers.

For example, just imagine the wide range of answers you'd get about what would be fair with respect to transferring a closely-held business interest if you were to ask each of the following:

a. The business owner

b. The business owner's spouse

c. The next generation currently working in the business

d. The spouse of the next generation currently working in the business

e. The next generation not currently working in the business

f. The key employee in the business

Although you are likely to get many different answers, none of them are necessarily wrong. It's important to appreciate that fairness is not solely objective, but can include subjective or qualitative elements that are hard to quantify.

This same issue may arise when you employ your child in the business.

Or if you have another child who is not in the business. Both children may want to follow a process that differs from each other or everyone else to arrive at a decision. Understand that this is not uncommon. However, it is important for the group, rather than a single person, to arrive at a process. When differences occur (and they will occur), I often suggest business owners go back to their determined values and principles and work from there.

One example I recently encountered dealt with the distribution policy of a very successful construction company. This company was an S corporation, so all of their net income was reported and tax was paid by the shareholder owners instead of the company. As a result, whether the company made a dividend distribution or not, the shareholders still had to report income and personally pay taxes on the income allocated to them.

As you can imagine, this could create potential problems for a shareholder who must pay tax on income they did not receive. As a result, this company agreed on a dividend distribution policy of 40% of the income. In other words, if the company made any income, it was required to distribute a minimum of 40% of its income to the shareholders regardless of the needs of the company.

As a shareholder who is not active in the business, your fairness lens may be set directly on the tax liability you might incur from the income of a business. In other words, you are likely to feel such a policy is fair because no shareholder should have to pay tax on the income they never receive.

However, in this situation, the non-shareholder CFO was concerned that the company ought not to be forced to make such a distribution. The company may encounter a need for liquidity, or a bank may try to restrict distribution due to certain bank covenants. The CFO felt a better process was to avoid forcing a set percentage of cash from the company to be in the form of a dividend. Rather, the CFO felt the decision should be made by the board on an annual basis after taking into consideration all the facts and circumstances the business is facing at that time.

I would suggest both the outside shareholder and CFO were correct in their concerns. As a shareholder, I myself would be anxious about paying my taxes associated with the income of the company. But as the CFO, I think it is also reasonable to be concerned about the liquidity of the company. Here is what these different views illustrate: you are going to run into different views no matter what. That's why it is important to address these issues ahead of time so you can better plan and ensure people don't feel they have been unfairly treated down the road.

Process Fairness Versus Outcome Fairness

As a business owner, you know all too well that the outcome of a decision is not always what you expect. In business as in life, while we have control over our decisions, we don't have control over the outcomes of said decisions.

This also proves true when it comes to trying to make fair business decisions. Although your process of coming to a decision about distribution may be fair, you can still end up with a very unfair outcome. Because of this, it's more important to be concerned about your process itself rather than the outcome of the process.

For instance, I once represented a business owner who had both a number of businesses, as well as wealth outside of these businesses. He knew he was dying, and he wanted to be fair to his three children. In an effort to be fair, he decided to divide his estate equally to each child. However, in deciding how to divide his estate, he chose to give his eldest son the business and his other children the other assets. He explained to them that he felt this son was the best person to run the company and that he did not wish to involve the other siblings as minority owners. He told them he felt this was the fairest way to secure each of their economic futures.

At the time, the children who did not get any of the business assets felt they had not been treated fairly, although they were richly rewarded with other assets. However, a few years later, as the result of some grave problems the father left behind in the business, the business the oldest son had received became almost worthless. At the same time, the assets his other children had received from their father continued to appreciate. In retrospect, I am sure the eldest son would have much preferred to receive the other assets rather than the declining business his father gave him.

As this story serves to remind us, we can seldom control the outcome, only the process.

When Should we Develop a Process for Determining Fairness?

As a business owner, you may choose to ignore fairness as part of your decision-making process. This is your right and prerogative. However, if you are a business owner who does decide to add fairness into your succession planning process, I recommend you develop a process for certain fundamental issues involved in a business. The more you can address these issues in advance and determine how your business will deal with them, the less likely someone will argue at a later date that they have been treated unfairly.

A closely-held business owner may wish to consider following a decision-making process when dealing with four significant matters. These four significant matters are as follows:

a. Selecting a leader or the CEO

b. Determining compensation

c. Deciding on a dividend policy

d. Deciding on the transfer of ownership

These four succession planning issues are so fundamental that you really do want to be sure that you've developed a decision-making process that is seen as fair and reasonable by all. Without a deliberate process, I have found that regardless of the outcome, someone will almost always argue that they have not been treated fairly. One the other hand, if you develop a decision-making process in advance that takes into account everyone's views, those who might not like the outcome will at least appreciate the fairness of how the decision was made.

Other Challenges to Fairness in Succession Planning

Besides the four fundamental succession planning issues covered above, there are other succession issues a business owner may want to consider in the process of a transition. Here are a few of those other issues you might run into:

a. You plan to transfer your business to the child who is currently active in the business. However, the value of the business greatly exceeds the value of the rest of your estate. How will you decide to divide the rest of your estate for the non-active family members?

b. You have had one child active in your business for years. They have become invaluable to the business. Should you exclude a portion of the value of your business that is attributable to the efforts of the active child? How will you measure that contribution? Will you use objective performance factors to determine the value attributable to the active child? How will you communicate that process to the active child as well as those who are not active in the business?

c. When you own a business, it is sometimes beneficial for estate and income tax planning purposes to transfer a portion of the business to the next generation of family members active in the business. However, you may not want to transfer other assets outside the business because you expect to use those assets for retirement. As a result, the non-active next generation must wait longer to receive their inheritance. You will need to weigh the value of estate and income tax planning against how you can be fair to other family members.

These are just a few of the issues that you may be faced with. I am certain there will be more. Of course, you can always make a decision on your own, without the input of others, rather than following the 5 steps I outlined above. However, be careful with big decisions like these because the way you deal with them and communicate them will almost certainly impact the success (or failure) of your transition plan.

Governance Fosters Fairness

What happens when a difficult decision needs to be made and you don't have a defined decision-making process? How does one operate a closely-held business fairly? One thing that almost always guarantees that everyone feels they have been treated fairly is making sure your company has a strong governance structure. I have found, time and time again, that when a company has a good governance structure, most family members, employees, and even in-laws will respect decisions made by the board.

Generally, good governance starts with an active board of directors. Research shows that most successfully-run closely-held businesses have an active board of directors. Beyond this, many of these companies also have independent directors on the board who are not employees, shareholders, or family members. When a board contains independent board members, there is at the very least a perception of objectivity in the decision-making process.

When a difficult issue arises and a decision may be challenged, it is often helpful to have a strong and active board. After all, one of a board's responsibilities is to deal with challenging issues. When such an issue is brought before the board, the board should (i) develop a decision-making process, (ii) do its due diligence, and (iii) ultimately come to a decision.

Fairness as a Tool or a Weapon

In summary, you can either use fairness as a tool or allow it to be used as a weapon against you. When used properly, creating a fair decision-making process can be a useful tool in deciding fundamental succession and business issues. If you develop a process in advance to decide on particular issues (such as the succession of the next CEO, compensation, or a dividend policy) and gain consensus in the process, it's unlikely that anyone will argue that the decision was unfair.

Alternatively, when a fundamental decision is made without the least perception of a fair process, anyone who feels negatively treated will likely disagree with the result. In these situations, they will use fairness as a weapon against you by arguing, "This is unfair" or "I have not been treated fairly." I've seen this play out enough times that I can confirm that this is not a position you want to be in nor an argument you want to have.

Here's what it all boils down to: good companies anticipate future events to avoid conflict later and ensure confidence within the group. When individuals understand that a decision was made following a defined process with consistency and certainty, fairness becomes a valuable tool for the business owner.

Keys to Chapter

1. Appreciate the differences between equal and fair. Fair may be equal, but equal may not be fair.

2. Develop a set process for making fair decisions on fundamental succession issues to improve the chances that your decision will be respected.

3. Acknowledge the different lens of fairness. Like beauty, fairness is in the eye of the beholder.

4. Understand the difference between the fairness of a process vs. the fairness of an outcome.

5. Good governance can go a long way in helping with the perception of a decision being fair.

BRADLEY J. FRANC

Part III: Succession Solution Tool Kit

CHAPTER EIGHT: THE SUCCESSION SOLUTION℠

"Planning is bringing the future into the present so that you can do something about it now."

–Alan Lakein

The Importance of Process

Nick Saban, head coach at the University of Alabama, has won more national collegiate football championships than any active coach. During his time at Louisiana State University (LSU), he developed what has come to be called "the Process," or process thinking. Back at LSU, Saban knew a football play lasted only a few seconds. This is not a very long period of time for a player to know how to respond. As a result, Saban developed a system or process for each player. Instead of worrying or thinking about the outcome of a particular play, Saban instructed each player to focus on a specific task or job. Saban broke down each position into specific tasks to be performed during the play. The player was instructed that if he focused on completing his task, a positive outcome would likely follow.[21] As the saying goes, the rest was history.

As in sports, most successful businesses have their own unique processes. In fact, it is often these unique processes that set them apart from their competition. For instance, The Four Seasons has hundreds of unique processes to improve the hotel experience it offers its customers. Likewise, Southwest Airlines has its own process for controlling costs and seat assignments. McDonald's, too, has hundreds of processes its employees follow to deliver the same tasting product, regardless of the location of the particular restaurant. (This one I know from personal experience, as it was my first job in high school.)

In a similar fashion, you need to follow a process to have an effective succession plan. Because succession planning addresses so many issues and impacts a variety of different stakeholders, you need a process that identifies, discusses, and tries to resolves these issues.

Any process you decide to follow should produce three outcomes: (i) clarity, (ii) simplicity and (iii) certainty. For instance, the process should produce a clear vision and clear steps you will pursue to achieve your desired results. The process must also be simple to follow and implement. Importantly, simple does not mean easy. Any effective succession process will take time and work to take the complex and find simplicity. But, as Albert Einstein once said, "If you can't explain it simply, do it simply, design it simply; it is because you don't understand it well enough". Finally, if the process you follow is both clear and simple, you, along with the other important stakeholders, will be certain as to what you are all trying to achieve.

The Succession Solution℠ is one such process to achieve a clear, simple and certain succession plan. The process helps you to clearly develop your unique goals with the use of a simple one-page form. Once created, the form provides certainty to those involved as to how you will accomplish your plan.

The Succession Solution℠ is designed to help you identify your purpose, discover where you are now, and confront challenges as you envision and enact your unique succession plan. Further, it is a process that can be used to monitor, direct, and amend your plan when necessary, as you assess and reassess what is best for both your company's and your future.

I've learned over many years and many diverse clients that most challenges can be overcome by identifying and following a logical process to achieve a positive result. As author Anthony Greenback states, "To live through an impossible situation, you don't need the reflexes of a Grand Prix driver, the muscles of a Hercules, or the mind of an Einstein; you simply need to know what to do."[22]

There are few problems that have not already been addressed by somebody or solved in some way. Whether the issue is how best to hire a key employee, generate more sales, raise capital, or sell a business, there are processes and solutions already in place that can be researched and followed. Plenty of procedures have been developed by experts to confront business challenges, and when adapted for individual situations and carefully pursued, they usually return a positive effect.

This is the reason why you pay lawyers, accountants, plumbers, electricians, and other professionals to give you advice. They have seen a variety of problems and typically have a proven solution. Unfortunately, when it comes to succession planning, there is a lot of talk about obstacles, but not much focus on a process for solutions.

Following a well-defined process generally leads to a successful solution, and the reason for this is two-fold. First, solutions are typically developed by experts in a particular area who have identified the top issues to address and the landmines to avoid when tackling a particular problem. Second, efficiency is often heightened by using a process. When a proven process is applied, time isn't wasted by developing your own process. In other words, you don't need to reinvent the wheel.

The Succession Solution℠ is the culmination of decades of trial and error in the field of succession planning. The process it describes leads to solutions by helping you uncover and address almost all of the important issues you will face when seeking a succession plan. Of course, no single process can address *all* business issues—the situations and needs of business owners are varied and unique. However, if you can address 80 percent of the issues before you, then it is a major accomplishment. This one-page succession solution is the tool you need to attain your goal.

The design of The Succession Solution℠ is based on the saying that progress that is measured improves, but progress that is measured and reported, improves exponentially! The tool offers complete flexibility, allowing you to design, monitor, and amend your succession plan to fit your unique and changing business. Moreover, the one-page succession tool contains a built-in monitoring feature that is central to its design. It is this embedded review and report system that makes The Succession Solution℠ a state-of-the-art succession-planning tool. Every ninety days, you and your key stakeholders reassess the plan, until you agree it has been successfully accomplished.

The one-page Succession Solution℠ has been refined over the years to ensure that business owners in a wide variety of industries can use it successfully, making it universally user-friendly. There is no reason to doubt that if you follow the steps outlined in this book, as well as consult a facilitator and other seasoned professionals, you can accomplish a successful solution on your own.

Although the approach outlined in this book is effective and proven to work, it is by no means the only process available. It is up to you which process you choose, but the important thing is that you select a succession plan approach and stick with it until you decide it does not work for you. As I've emphasized earlier, if you decide an approach is not working, please don't stop the process. Rather, seek another approach until you find one that works. If you decide not to pursue any process, you risk both your business and the family relationships that will be impacted by the loss of your business. I can tell you that when a family business is lost from one generation to another, family relationships can be destroyed beyond repair. This is why it is so important to begin—and to follow—a proven succession process.

The Succession Solution℠ approach is distinctive because it addresses practically everything you need in order to generate and execute an effective succession plan in a single page. Moreover, when consistently followed, it becomes a roadmap to success. I have come across many succession plans that possess the correct philosophy but lack an executable method. I have seen just as many plans that focus only on the needs of the business owner, but don't address the fundamental needs of the family, the business, or the employees. If you follow the one-page Succession Solution℠, however, your chances of achieving a successful transition will be greatly enhanced.

Succession Process: Case Study

Many years ago, I was hired by a successful real estate developer to help him with his company's succession plan. He had started his company with nothing but his tool-belt and what he knew as a carpenter. He would often refer to himself as "nothing but a dumb carpenter," but few people who knew him would have labeled him that way. On the contrary, this gentleman was one of the wisest and most insightful men I knew.

He owned a prosperous company with a substantial net worth that would be subject to significant federal and state taxes upon his death. The problem with many clients like this is that they have a very large estate, but little liquidity. Additional stress is added to the situation when a bank debt is associated with a closely-held company, like developers. Many times, when a founder passes away, the bank's loan documents require that the loan go into immediate default. When the liabilities of death taxes are coupled with the immediate collection of bank debt, it's easy to understand why so many closely-held businesses fail after a founder passes.

This business owner had the same concerns. He was fearful that upon his death the company would be forced into sale at a liquidation price to pay the tax and bank liabilities associated with his passing. At the conclusion of my initial meeting, I recommended that we follow The Succession Solution℠ process. I explained that we needed to (i) decide why he wanted to undertake a succession planning process, (ii) determine what was currently in place, (iii) identify the risks for his plan, (iv) engage other important stakeholders, and (v) develop both long-term and short-term goals. Fortunately, the client agreed to follow the process.

Even though he agreed to follow a process, however, he remained reluctant to start. A variety of concerns and fears were preventing him from making any progress on his succession plan, including making any transfers of ownership to his children. In a candid conversation, the client admitted he did not want to lose control of his company, and it became apparent to me that the company had become his identity. He feared that by transferring full ownership to his children, all could be lost. What if they were to marry and get divorced? What if, after marriage, one of his children passed away? Would he then be forced into business with an in-law he did not want to work with? Could a transfer of wealth to his children backfire by destroying their will to work? He was also concerned about his daughter, who was not active in the business. He wanted to try to treat everyone as fairly as possible. I assured the client that these were all very common concerns in a family business.

After several meetings with both the client and his business-involved children, we developed a plan to address nearly every concern. After a few more meetings, the client realized that the potential negative results of not planning were much worse than what he would encounter if he started a planning process he could control and direct. Once he came to this realization, most of his anxieties diminished. The family finally decided to slowly transfer ownership to all three of the developer's children. Although one child was not active in the business, the other two siblings agreed to buy out the non-active sibling upon their father's passing.

Once we started the planning process, which included the transfer of some ownership, the impact on the founder, his children, and his business was so beneficial that he requested I automatically repeat the process every year. Today, the founder still has management control of some of his companies, but he has transferred most of those companies to his children. What's more, he is so pleased with the process that he's now speaking to his adult children about continuing the planning he began twenty years earlier. As you might imagine, the founder's children have embraced the father's recommendations, because they've seen how well succession planning works.

Common Fears to Overcome

Closely-held business owners are not any different from most people. Before starting anything new like a succession plan, you are likely to experience certain fears and anxieties. Fear is part of being human. Indeed, it was our fears and hesitations that protected us thousands of years ago in the face of very different yet equally real threats. While you will have your own unique set of facts and concerns specific to your business, there are six fears I see most often that prevent the start of a succession plan.

1. Fear of the Unknown

Because many business owners have little experience in the succession process, they have no idea what can happen. In the face of a novel experience, we probably unconsciously resurrect the anxieties produced by the many scary movies we've all seen. We know our hero is about to be clobbered when he or she turns that corner in the dark and scary room. Similarly, at the start of succession planning, business owners fear that they just don't know what the process has in store.

2. Fear of Commitment

Many business owners don't like to give up control, and they fear this will be the inevitable result of succession planning. As we have seen, however, adaptations are possible with any succession planning process.

3. Fear of Self-Exposure

Creating a lucrative business is an extraordinary accomplishment. However, each of us has certain strengths and weaknesses. Many business owners fear exposing their weaknesses, and with an unknown process like succession planning looming before them, fear of exposure is easily exacerbated.

4. Fear of Failure

This may be the most common fear among business owners. No one likes to fail, especially a successful business owner. It is natural not to want to fail. However, I once heard that the reason we fall is to learn how to get up. Too many people are afraid to start something new because they fear failure. Imagine how the world might change if more of us believed failure could be a productive rather than paralyzing process?

5. Fear of the Imperfect

Many successful business owners became prosperous because they knew how to "sweat the details." They worked hard to build a productive company, and now they imagine that their succession plan must achieve instant perfection. Thus, if they can't envision an immediate and perfect solution, they simply decide that now is not the time for succession planning.

6. Fear of Succeeding

It may seem paradoxical to fear success, especially for thriving businesses, but I have often seen it emerge among successful business owners. While it may surprise you, the complexity of this fear keeps it hidden. As demonstrated in the case study above, a business owner may have his or her identity and life purpose so wrapped up in the company that an effective succession planning process signals an existential loss of self and meaning. Thus, the business owner actually fears success in the succession plan. I had one retiring CEO tell me that he feared going from, "he is the man" to "who is he?"

An Antidote to Fear: Engaging the Four C's

As mentioned earlier in the chapter, fear was holding back the real estate developer from taking action. Only after we identified and addressed each fear did we really begin to make progress on his succession plan.

Dan Sullivan, creator of The Strategic Coach® Program, a coaching program for entrepreneurs, developed a concept called The Four C's Formula®. It is a simple but powerful model to address fear. Sullivan explains how to take on an opportunity or obligation and achieve the result you seek. The Four C's stand for Commitment, Courage, Capability, and Confidence, and I suggest you incorporate the Four C's concept as you begin your succession planning.

The first C stands for commitment. Before you undertake any opportunity, challenge, or obligation, the first thing you must do is make a commitment. A commitment involves dedicating yourself to a person or a cause. In your case, the commitment is to take on the challenge and the opportunity of the succession planning process. Without a commitment, you will fail at the first roadblock, detour, or problem you encounter.

It is impossible to build a viable succession plan without commitment.

In fact, if you start a succession plan without the commitment to see it through, you are likely to create more damage than good.

The second C stands for courage. Most opportunities that present themselves involve some fears and risks on the road to achievement. As a business owner, you take on risk almost every day, whether it is hiring a new employee, buying new equipment, or entering a new market. And you take on those risks after assessing likely outcomes. You recognize there is a risk associated with the challenge, yet you proceed, because of the associated pay-off.

One risk may be addressing a family relationship you are hesitant to address. You may also fear risking the money and/or time you will need to see a succession plan through to a successful conclusion. Succession planning is risky, because its outcome is not 100 percent guaranteed, but you wouldn't be a successful entrepreneur if you were too afraid to take risks.

The third C stands for capability. Once you have made the commitment, mustered the courage to assume the risks, and worked through your plan, you (and your important stakeholders) develop the capability to effectively complete your succession plan.

The last of the four Cs is confidence. Once you have completed the first three steps and begun to implement your succession plan, you and your entire team will gain a new confidence, because you will have a clear path forward for your company. This is one of the most rewarding aspects of succession planning. Witnessing the confidence business owners gain after generating and implementing their succession plan is one of the greatest rewards one can obtain as an adviser.

It is the Start That Often Stops You

Fear often prevents business owners from beginning the succession planning process. As Hall of Fame football coach Don Shula once said, "It's the start that stops most people." You can't let fear stop you from starting the succession planning process. It is especially important to identify the specific fears that are holding you back and examine them unflinchingly.

The Succession Solution^{SM} will help you address your doubts and anxieties. Once you start working toward a goal, you will realize that you can complete the task. As Zig Ziglar once said, "A goal properly set is halfway reached." Even if you complete only 50 percent, 60 percent, or 70 percent of your goal, you will be that much further ahead than if you had not tried at all. If you were to meet someone a year from today, and you could tell them you have already made 50 percent, 60 percent, or 70 percent progress on your succession plan, wouldn't you feel good about this scenario? I can promise that, no matter how far you get, if you work through the succession process, you will be further along than if you do nothing. What do you have to lose but a few hours of your time?

The Succession Solution℠ Process

The Succession Solution℠ is a carefully designed process to help you answer (i) *Why* you want to do this, (ii) *What* fears or obstacles you need to overcome, (iii) *How* you will overcome those obstacles, and (iv) *When* you will overcome them and achieve your succession plan.

What's more, as I often find when working with clients, new ideas emerge during the planning process that you would never have considered otherwise. It is like walking down a hallway: doors begin to appear and open that you could never have seen or predicted had you remained standing still.

Keys to Chapter

1. Most things in life and nature follow a process. Succession planning is one of those tasks that lend to following a process to achieve a desired result.

2. The use of a process allows efficiency and effectiveness, and the determination of achieving one's defined goals.

3. Once your succession task is identified, accepted, encountered, and completed, you, your team, and your company will be stronger and better prepared for the next challenge.

CHAPTER NINE: USING THE SUCCESSION SOLUTION℠

> "He who chooses the beginning of the road chooses the place it leads to."
>
> – Henry David Thoreau

The Succession Solution℠ takes you through six separate but interrelated stages. Each stage is designed to build the foundation for the next stage until the process is complete, and each stage has been separately defined based on its objective. The design also requires that you work through each stage fully before moving on to the next. The names of each stage are as follows: *The Purpose Stage, The Discovery Stage, The Challenge Stage, The Mission Stage, The Annual Stage* and *The Quarterly Stage.* Completing the sequential steps offered by this tool will provide the confidence and direction you and your team will need to execute an effective succession plan. Like many well-developed planning systems, The Succession Solution℠'s whole is greater than the sum of its parts.

I like to compare the process to pouring concrete. Once the concrete is set and allowed to properly dry, it becomes extremely hard and capable of holding a tremendous amount of pressure. However, if you try to build on concrete that is not set or completely cured, it will crumble like blue cheese. Like solid concrete, The Succession Solution℠ will act as your company's foundation as it handles the loads and pressures placed upon it during the execution of your succession plan.

Before working through the stages, however, there is some preliminary work to accomplish: establishing an agreed upon business name; clearly articulating your business's primary activity; identifying the major stakeholders; and setting a date. Below I explain in detail each of these beginning steps.

Business Name or Names

Let's begin with a simple but important question. Ask each member in the planning group the name of your company. You may find this step a bit bizarre, but I have found that people often use multiple names to refer to a single organization. Asking this question from the start is a unifying strategy, and it ensures that everyone is on the same page. It is a good exercise to pull everyone's thoughts about your company together, and I advise that before proceeding, you achieve consensus on your company's name.

Business Activity

Next, invite everyone around the table to describe the business activity of your organization. Depending on your business, you may get a few different answers. Some may think your company provides a service, while others believe it provides a product. Of course, some companies offer a variety of services and activities. Nonetheless, it is important to reach a consensus about your company's primary activity. If you understand and agree upon what service or product your company provides, your team will be better equipped to determine what is needed to move it forward to the next group of managers. Additionally, if you get stuck on a particular stage during the planning process, referring back to this activity may help you advance to the next stage.

Obviously, if key stakeholders hold different views about your company's primary activity, it would only be natural that they would have different views on how best to plan for its succession. If one stakeholder thinks that your organization provides a service, while another thinks it is product based, their views of who is fit to become the next leader may differ fundamentally.

While holding different views does not make one stakeholder right over another, problems can arise when stakeholders can't reach a common ground on your company's main activity. When you define the business together as a preliminary step, however, you are better prepared to determine the appropriate succession solution for your company. For instance, someone who has an operational background in manufacturing may not be the initial choice for CEO if the company is moving toward a service sector.

I was recently hired to work for a business with three equal owners. I had already been providing legal advice to the firm for more than fifteen years, and we had successfully transitioned one prior owner. At this point, however, the current owners were struggling over a succession plan. It was a prosperous company, but when independent discussions stalled, the owners realized they needed to undertake a defined succession plan. Moreover, they worried that, by selling the business to a third party, they may not receive the value they needed to retire. They knew that in five-to-ten years they would want to begin developing a new generation of leaders. As a result of these shared concerns and values, the owners were considering hiring a chief operating officer, and they decided to go through the succession planning process to achieve this goal.

At our initial meeting, I asked each owner to describe the company's main activity. To my surprise, I received three different answers. One described the business as a distributor to the construction industry; another defined the business as a manufacturer's representative; and the third labeled it as a manufacturing company. Interestingly, I discerned that the reason for these three different answers had to do with the three separate areas in which each owner worked.

You can imagine the difficulty in hiring a COO as the next logical step. What type of COO would the company have sought? How would the current owners have described the job and/or the primary activity of the company? Happily, by the time our plan was finished, the owners had agreed on the main activity of the company, and we were in a much better position to develop a job description.

Once you agree on the primary activity of your business, you set the necessary foundation for completing your plan. Verifying your defined business activity allows you to assess, validate, establish, and reassess your long-and short-term goals. What's more, I advise you not to rush through this first step, because it could jeopardize the entire succession planning process.

Major Stakeholders

The Chinese philosopher Confucius once said, "I hear I forget, I see I remember, I do I understand."

This quote supports The Succession Solution^{SM}'s emphasis on the active involvement of major stakeholders in the succession planning process. It is natural to identify all major stakeholders before working through the stages. Including a stakeholder on your list, however, does not equate to accommodating that individual's every whim. Instead, the goal is to involve all major stakeholders in the learning process. This will also improve the likelihood of acceptance for stakeholders; a person is more likely to agree with and adopt an idea if they are involved in the process.

Identifying and listing your company's significant stakeholders does not mean that you'll invite each stakeholder into the planning session. You identify important stakeholders during the process, so you can consider the plan's impact on them throughout the assessment process. You are likely to face some challenging decisions as you work through your succession planning process, and if you keep your major stakeholders in mind, you will be better prepared to deal with them. Of course, you can complete this form on your own, but I recommend greater involvement.

Deciding whom to invite into this process will be critical to its success, and it is better to err on the side of more inclusion rather than less. However, just because someone is listed as a major stakeholder does not mean they are qualified to join the planning team. If you think an individual does not understand the importance of succession planning, or might try to derail the process, then it is best to exclude them.

You may be confronted with challenging team members. A technique I use to deal with this situation is to invite the team member to form a committee to resolve the contested issue. This gesture alone is often enough to transform the difficult team member from recalcitrant obstructer to productive problem solver. People normally appreciate when they've been heard, and once they're materially involved in the problem-solving process, they don't want to fail.

The bottom line is that you'll dramatically increase the success rate of your plan if you bring the right stakeholders into the planning process. Not only will the task itself be easier for not having to do it alone, but you'll already have significant buy-in when it comes time to announce and implement the plan.

Another value realized from inviting more people to the planning process comes from the delegation of work. The Succession Solution℠ demands the completion of a series of tasks each calendar quarter, so if you decide to develop the plan on your own, you risk becoming overwhelmed. However, if you have several stakeholders in the meeting, you can delegate some of these duties to them. Additionally, the more ownership in the process you afford to stakeholders, the more you increase the plan's probability of success.

I would also strongly suggest, if possible, that you consider engaging a third party to help facilitate the process. While I have seen The Succession Solution℠ completed successfully without the help of an outside facilitator, I think it works better with a third party onboard. In my experience, when you bring a third-party facilitator to a family planning meeting the participants are more respectful of the process. Members are more likely to follow the direction and instructions of a third party than they are to obey a sibling, parent, or other relative. Moreover, bringing in a third party often allows for tougher questions to be asked, because a family member may be hesitant to raise sensitive issues.

When a facilitator is engaged, participants who do not hold a leadership position often find the process to be without as much bias. Conversely, when you lead the process, other contributors may feel the plan has already been developed and the meeting is being held only to announce what you have already decided. An outside perspective can be very helpful in identifying blind spots that no one in the family has been able to see or is reluctant to address.

Important stakeholders typically include significant owners in your business, key employees, or family members who will be materially impacted by a change in leadership. Only after deciding the type of planning required, however, will you be able to choose who should be invited. For instance, if you are discussing a change in management, you might limit the meeting to those actively involved in the business, rather than including non-active, non-working owners. On the other hand, if you are discussing a sale or transfer of the business to the next generation, you may want to consider including family members who will be impacted by the change.

Regardless of whom you decide to include, the primary test for inclusion should be the stakeholder's willingness to bring a positive, productive, and open mind to the process. If you feel someone will not be able to adopt this approach, you may want to seriously consider how best to exclude him or her.

The question of whether or not an individual stakeholder has the capacity to understand the succession planning process may give cause for concern. Of course, this does not mean that the stakeholder's concerns should be overlooked. If you solicit even the uninformed stakeholders' thoughts and concerns—even outside the actual planning meetings—you will be in a better position to achieve success than if you ignore them. Once ignored, a stakeholder feels disenfranchised, and they may try to upset the process or challenge the result.

Deciding who to include in the succession planning process allows you to have a real impact on your relationships with family members, and even to learn something new. Although a particular family member may not be included or interested in your business, you can still explain the importance of The Succession Solution℠ for your business's success, as well as seek that member's input. Asking for a particular person's views and thoughts, even though he or she may not be invited to the process, can be a strong strategy. Remember, though, that when you seek the counsel of a non-invited member, it's important to return to that person and explain the results of the process and why you arrived at your particular plan.

Remember, too, that even though the thought of tackling a sensitive issue or uncovering a personal family matter makes you uncomfortable, it will *not* go away just because you avoid the subject and/or concern. Instead, these problems and disputes are likely to resurface later and carry with them even more emotional baggage. Rather than evading difficulties, you must afford troubled stakeholders the time and space needed to air their concerns. Allowing family members to vent their concerns is enough to show them that you care.

I recall a succession planning process in which I helped a very successful business owner who had only two of his three children involved in the business. The other had gainful independent employment. One of the owner's sons had done a great job running and growing the business for over twenty years, and he was clearly the next leader. The other son, while competent, did not have the leadership qualities of his sibling. Because the father had a very difficult time trying to be as fair as possible, little succession planning was being accomplished. This created tension and angst between the siblings and parents. I can still recall some very emotional moments during the process. However, the father knew he had to make a difficult decision. As the saying goes, there is no good way to deliver bad news. Eventually, we all met with the two siblings and discussed the transition of a majority stake in the ownership, along with management control to the heir apparent.

In order to protect the father's income from the company, as well as the one sibling not chosen to the lead the company, we created agreements to ensure certain family expectations were met during their employment, as well as protections if the company was ever sold by the new CEO/majority shareholder. While delivering the initial news was difficult, I think everyone knew it was the correct decision. Fortunately, the new CEO knew his responsibility and ran the company successfully for over a decade, until the family received a terrific offer to sell the company. In the end, due to the agreement we put in place, everyone was richly rewarded and satisfied with the resolution.

When faced with a sensitive family matter, you may ask a stakeholder for recommendations to address his or her concerns about The Succession Solution^{SM} planning process. Asking for a solution is often much better than imposing a result. I have found that when you take a servant-leader approach, you gain much more respect than acting like a dictator.

Seeking input from others shows respect. When you keep an open mind, you can discover unsuspected truths about your family or business. More importantly, family members who have a strong relationship with one another can disagree and still know their relationships are strong. You need to let family members know you can dislike their ideas and still love them very much. Hopefully, teaching family members the importance of The Succession Solution℠ process instills the necessary trust to facilitate the initial procedure and ensure it goes even better the next time and/or when a crisis occurs.

Clearly, you benefit by connecting with all major stakeholders prior to the initial planning meeting to obtain counsel and input from each. Once a stakeholder's input is received, you should solicit each person's biggest concern, while simultaneously making it clear that even though a stakeholder's input is important, it will not dictate or control the process. Again, when people understand their role and how their input will be used, better outcomes follow.

I have discovered that education is the best way to deal with uninformed stakeholders. If a stakeholder is open to the process, he or she should be receptive to education and information. One helpful approach is to have a non-family member meet with the stakeholder to explain the situation or business in detail. Once a stakeholder has been educated and given an opportunity to share, you can then decide if the stakeholder is really interested in helping, or just being difficult. When you make a genuine effort to educate and include a stakeholder, and he or she continues to be difficult, it is time to move forward without them. At least you and other members of the process will know that you've made a sincere effort to address the concerns of all main stakeholders.

As stated earlier in this chapter, while it is critical to identify and include impacted stakeholders, it does not mean they necessarily have an equal voice in the process, or that they can dictate the ultimate plan. Rather, you should include stakeholders in the succession planning process just as you would in making other important business decisions. Typically, when making an important decision, you will consult your CEO, CFO, CPA, lawyer, banker, and/or insurance representative. It is a rare occurrence, however, for each of these advisers to agree on the same recommendation. Thus, after meeting with these advisers and considering their advice, it is you who must ultimately make the final decision.

As I have said, in addition to the practice of law, I have created four separate companies over the last thirty years. The industries involved included real estate, personnel staffing, and technology, and two of these companies achieved recognition nine separate times from *Inc.* as a fastest growing company. Even so, I have a confession to make. At various times during the life of my companies, I made business decisions I would not have made as a lawyer or a CPA. In fact, some of my decisions were in conflict with the views of several of my important stakeholders. I made those decisions, however, based on all the information I knew at the time. I suspect you may have done the same. Take that same view when going through the succession planning process. Gain as much valuable information as you can, seek the advice and counsel of others, but in the end, know that you must make the hard call. This is why you are in the lead position.

Date (Staying on Track)

Don't forget to date your form. The Succession Solution℠ will become your historic document, and you will want to recall when you started the process. While this step may appear basic, you will be glad you did it.

Since many of your goals and objections will be date specific, establish the date on which you began and when you updated each step of the process. These dates will allow you to hold others accountable, both to the goals and the date by which they will be accomplished. A deadline can be a powerful motivation.

The Succession Solution℠ Worksheet

Refer to Illustration 9.1 for the Succession Solution Worksheet to review. Once completed, the worksheet becomes an organic document which provides direction, focus, and accountability in the execution of your succession plan. You'll complete The Succession Solution Worksheet at the beginning of the planning process, and then return to it again at future planning meetings.

It will usually take you and your team longer to complete the worksheet the first time around than it will at subsequent meetings. This is because the first time requires laying the foundation of your succession plan, which you will likely not change at subsequent meetings. Typically, the first three stages of the worksheet will remain as you completed them in the beginning, while you will make changes and amendments to the last three stages later down the road.

From Chapter Ten on, I have included the appropriate stage of the worksheet to review in order to provide an example of a completed stage. You will find an example of a completed worksheet in the appendix at the end of the book.

Illustration 9.1 – The Succession Solution℠ Worksheet

Purpose

1. What are the Core Principles of Stakeholders?

- ______
- ______
- ______
- ______
- ______

2. What is the Ultimate Succession Plan Vision? (Find your North Star)

- ______
- ______
- ______
- ______
- ______

3. Why? (Does Vision Align with Core Principles?)

- ______
- ______
- ______
- ______
- ______
- ______
- ______

4. What Does Failure Look Like?

- ______
- ______
- ______
- ______
- ______

Discovery

5. Where are we now and what is in place for succession?

(Where is the Red Dot?)

(Management, Ownership, Employees, Family Dynamics)

- ______
- ______
- ______
- ______
- ______
- ______

Challenge

6. Strengths

- ______
- ______
- ______
- ______
- ______
- ______

7. Opportunities

- ______
- ______
- ______
- ______
- ______
- ______

8. Obstacles

- ______
- ______
- ______
- ______
- ______
- ______

9. Strategies for Overcoming Obstacles

- ______
- ______
- ______
- ______
- ______
- ______
- ______

Reporter: ______ Meeting Date: ______

Business Name: ______________ Business Activity: ______________
Initiation Date: ______________

Mission (3 Years)	Annual Review	Quarterly Review	
10. Goals • ______ • ______ • ______ • ______ • ______ • ______	**14.** Goals • ______ • ______ • ______ • ______ • ______ • ______	**18.** 90 days	Resp. Pty
11. Obstacles • ______ • ______ • ______ • ______ • ______ • ______	**15.** Obstacles • ______ • ______ • ______ • ______ • ______ • ______		
12. Actions • ______ • ______ • ______ • ______ • ______ • ______	**16.** Actions • ______ • ______ • ______ • ______ • ______ • ______	**19.** Success Criteria • ______ • ______ • ______ • ______ • ______ • ______	
13. Measurements of Success (KPIs) • ______ • ______ • ______ • ______ • ______ • ______ • ______	**17.** Measurements of Success (KPIs) • ______ • ______ • ______ • ______ • ______ • ______ • ______	**20.** Celebration of Success • ______ **21.** Next Meeting Date • ______	

Download a printable version of this worksheet at **www.thesuccessionsolution.com/workbook.**

Keys to Chapter

1. The Succession Solution^{SM} is designed to set the foundation of your succession plan. Without a strong foundation, your plan may fail under the pressure you will encounter during the process.

2. The Succession Solution^{SM} has separate stages which build upon each stage, so it is important to go through each stage before proceeding to the next.

3. Identify and involve key stakeholders in the process to improve the likelihood of them accepting your plan.

CHAPTER TEN: THE PURPOSE STAGE

> "Lack of definite real purpose is the royal road to drifting, desertion, and derelict."
>
> – William George Jordan

Establishing Your Purpose

The initial stage in developing an effective succession plan is to establish your purpose for undertaking this task. Your purpose lays the groundwork for the entire project. While having a defined purpose may not guarantee your plan's success, if you lack a clear rationale for initiating your succession planning process, its absence will surely increase the likelihood of failure.

Defining your purpose allows you to explain your thought process to others as you make targeted decisions and develop key strategic moves. Keeping participants involved and informed as the succession process unfolds is an important dimension of any effective plan. Without a clear purpose for taking on these succession objectives, you and your team are likely to lose faith or become frustrated with the process midway through. In essence, your purpose is the bedrock for the entire succession process.

When developers construct large buildings, they design a foundation system that will support the weight and stress of the completed structure. Similarly, your purpose provides the strong and stable foundation you'll need to go the distance with your succession plan. Don't worry if your first attempt at developing your purpose is not perfect, because it will never be perfect. Trust that, as you move through the planning process, you will refine and improve your purpose as you adapt it to the needs of your specific objectives.

Although many of us may define purpose in slightly different ways, for the "purposes" of this book, I recommend you imagine your plan's rationale as a compass you will use to set your plan's direction, rather than as an isolated goal or destination to be reached. For example, your purpose may be to ensure the successful transition of your business to safeguard the wellbeing of customers, employees, community, and family. In contrast, your goal may be to find a new CEO, so you can spend time with your family. As you can see, the first succession planning purpose is much broader in scope than the second. Thinking of your purpose as a compass supports the vision from which all key stakeholders will benefit.

While you may not ultimately achieve your purpose, it will provide you and your team an ultimate destination or vision. As William George Jordan states in the *Power of Purpose*, "The great thing in life is not in realizing a purpose, but in fighting for it."[23]

What Are the Core Principles of the Primary Stakeholders?

The first step in the *Purpose Stage* of the one-page Succession Solution^{SM} is to determine the core principles or values you intend to follow during the succession process. Core values or principles represent the vital and guiding standards you've set for yourself and your company. What will be the central principles you'll follow as you undertake your succession plan, and when you face a challenge or problem along the way? For example, one core principle may be a commitment to showing respect for all stakeholders throughout the planning process. Another core principle may involve listening to and seeking input from all major stakeholders. While you may not agree or ultimately implement each stakeholder's perspective, by listening to all key stakeholders, you signal your pledge to gather and consider the views of others.

In a 2004 article by the *Economist*,[24] researchers showed that families whose businesses survive multiple generations operated on a set of agreed principles that pass from one generation to the next. The article goes on to state that these same principles should be used when debating over the broad direction of the company.

In 2015, the *Harvard Business Review (HBR)* examined what leadership lessons could be learned from great family businesses. The results of one acid test showed a commonality in corporate culture or ethics (otherwise known as principles or values). Remarkably, the *HBR* found a 95 percent overlap in the language that each family firm used to describe the company's culture. The words were respect, integrity, quality, humility, passion, modesty, and ambition. The *HBR* article went on to state that with the same values and vision, trust is formed.[25] I am not suggesting you use the same terms, but I do suggest you find a set of principles you can agree upon before proceeding too far in the succession planning process.

Many business owners come to succession planning with fundamental life principles already developed. The existence of these core values has contributed to your ongoing success, both personally and professionally. During the succession planning process, however, it is important for you, your family, and your key stakeholders to delineate your *shared* values and put them into writing. This collaborative activity can avert potential confusion down the road. Moreover, when the central purpose for undertaking a succession plan is determined collectively and rooted in the group's shared principles, the process can be motivating, enlightening, and productive.

Seeking input from others in the purpose stage of succession planning often leads to greater acceptance, insight, and unity in the development of a succession plan. This remains true even if the views and values of every stakeholder are not fully integrated into the plan. As discussed in chapter nine, when other members of your succession planning team genuinely feel they have been heard, it becomes easier for them to accept the plan's implementation. (Interestingly, this is true even if these members still believe their plan was better!)

The famous Holocaust survivor Viktor Frankl once observed, "Values do not drive a man; they do not push him, but rather pull him." Identifying core principles and values, both on your own and collaboratively—and writing them down—gives the team a document to return to at various times during the succession planning process. You will want and need such a record, especially when there is a conflict between key stakeholders. When a conflict does occur, the collaboratively-designed core principles can become a powerful unifying tool. Asking the group to test the dispute against the core principles can be a strong strategy. Ask the group if one of their core principles has been violated in the dispute. If you discover that the answer is yes, stop and determine how best to proceed. If you don't address the violation when it occurs, you risk losing the respect of the group and jeopardizing the process. Ultimately, using your shared purpose and core values will ease team members through difficulties and keep everyone's eyes on the larger goals.

What is Your Succession Plan Vision?

"If you don't know where you are going, you'll end up someplace else."
– **Yogi Berra**

There is a verse in the book of Proverbs that states, "Where there is no vision, the people perish."[26] The same can be said about a business. You must have a vision for your business, or it too will perish. In his book, *Legacy*, James Kerr puts it this way: "Vision without action is a dream. Action without vision is a nightmare."

Your vision becomes your line of sight. It provides you the direction you need to take and guidance when you need to adjust your journey due to a roadblock or obstacle encountered along the way. Your vision allows you to reset if you happen to go off course. Famed consultant Stephen Covey stated that the key to creativity is to begin with the end in mind—with a vision and a blueprint of the desired result.

After developing your core principles, you will want to develop your vision for the positive completion of your succession plan. At this stage of the discovery process, your vision statement should encompass your overall succession plan objectives. It is a statement of the ultimate goal or goals you want to accomplish over time, and it will serve as a clear guide for choosing current and future courses of action—those ultimate goals you want to achieve over the next five to ten years. You do not want to think short term at this point. In fact, you may have to accept that some elements of your vision will not be achieved until after you are gone.

In *Legacy*, James Kerr refers to an old proverb about a society that grows great when old men plant trees whose shade they will never see. When developing your goals, don't be afraid to think long term. Such thinking helps to eliminate those short-term challenges and constraints that so often prevent people from starting. Assume you have the ability to achieve your vision, and then record that vision. Constraints and time frames will be set and tackled later.

Remember that your vision should be aspirational at this point in the process. They should not be easily achieved. Instead, they will make demands on you and your team. Aspirational goals can be an excellent motivating force for your team. Ideally, your objectives will galvanize stakeholders, too, enticing them to engage with the process.

During this visionary exercise of succession planning, try to list as many goals as you would like to ultimately achieve. It is better to list more rather than fewer goals. When I am involved in a succession planning process, I usually challenge the group to think big. I tell them not to worry if the goals are too big, too substantial, or appear difficult to achieve. At this point in the process, you want all involved to challenge themselves to imagine without limits.

When you undertake this sort of free-form goal setting, I guarantee that you'll be pleasantly surprised by the creative ideas your team develops. What's more, the activity itself will provide great insight into the actual thinking processes of your group. While you may believe you already know how your team members think, this visionary step can be enlightening. There are no wrong answers during this phase of the discovery process. Unexpected perspectives and unconventional views are often brought to the foreground. There is one caveat, however, that I often insist upon—anyone who puts forth a visionary goal should also be able to articulate why they value that goal and how it agrees with the company's core principles.

Once all team members have had the opportunity to list their goals and the reasons they want to achieve them, the group needs to prioritize these goals. At this point, it's likely that some hard decisions will need to be made. You won't be able to achieve every imagined goal, so the team must decide on its top priorities. Of course, this narrowing will require some work and patience, but once the group has whittled down the list to the top three to five goals, you'll be ready to take the next step.

After delineating your top goals, you may realize that some of these goals conflict with others. This is not common, but when it happens you need to decide which goal should have priority over the other. This does not mean the less urgent goal should be disregarded or forgotten. Rather, you can agree to work on the lower-priority goals after realizing the goals with the highest priority.

As you already know, organizations have limited resources, not just financial, but time and even patience, too. How you allocate resources will impact the achievement of your goals. For instance, your goal might be to ensure there is enough capital to re-tool and re-capitalize equipment. However, a shareholder in your company who's not directly involved in your business might seek to maintain sufficient cash flow for investors. While separately each goal may seem fine to a particular group of stakeholders, together they can come into conflict. By prioritizing such goals, it is possible to bring your goals into alignment for the greater good of your company.

Although I have just encouraged casting wide-net goals, at this visionary phase of the purpose stage, I do like to challenge you and your team to identify your most important single goal. This is not to suggest that the other goals are less important than this single goal and will not be addressed. Instead, it's because I want you to discover and fully agree upon your organization's ultimate goal for initiating the succession planning process.

In the strategic planning world, some planners call this move "developing your BHAG"—your Big Hairy Audacious Goal!. The term BHAG was first created by international business consultants Jim Collins and Jerry Porras in their 1994 book, *Built to Last: Successful Habits of Visionary Companies*.

In most strategic planning processes, the development of a BHAG is fundamental. Without the BHAG, your company risks a lack of direction or clear focus. Without a clear sense of direction, it's impossible to generate the strong strategies necessary to get you through the process.

This is reminiscent of Alice's exchange with the Cheshire Cat in *Alice's Adventures in Wonderland*, where Alice begins by asking:

> "Would you tell me, please, which way I ought to go from here?"
>
> "That depends a good deal on where you want to get to," said the Cat.
>
> "I don't much care where—" said Alice.
>
> "Then it doesn't matter which way you go," said the Cat.
>
> "—so long as I get somewhere," Alice added as an explanation.
>
> "Oh, you're sure to do that," said the Cat, "if you only walk long enough."

As one who has done both strategic and succession planning for over twenty years, I think it's valid to compare both types of planning. I drew upon my knowledge of and experience with both types of planning to develop The Succession Solution℠. So, let me remind you again that as you establish your BHAG, don't be constrained by time frame or other factors. Even though you may never reach 100 percent of your BHAG, this goal will become your succession plan's North Star. Remember, a ship's captain sets a course using the North Star but never really intends to reach it. This does not make the North Star or the process itself a failure.

Strategic planner Dan Sullivan, when referring to the frustrations experienced by some business owners who can't achieve their ultimate vision, describes them as being caught in The Gap™. Sullivan uses the metaphor of rowing a boat toward a horizon when working to achieve a big goal.[27] While you may feel you are making progress, you can get frustrated when you look up and see the horizon just as far away as when you started. Sometimes, even when you are making terrific progress on a goal, it can be frustrating to see and acknowledge how much farther there is to go to reach the goal's achievement. What's more, by the time you achieve one big goal, you've often already set sail toward another! Thus, I encourage you to use your ultimate goal as a horizon or North Star, but not to get caught in The Gap. Once you and your team develop the ultimate goal, chances of a positive completion increase dramatically.

Why Do You Want to Achieve This Purpose?

"He who has a why to live for can bear with almost any how." These words are Friedrich Nietzsche's,[28] and they are pertinent at this phase of the succession planning process. Determining *why* you want to achieve your purpose may be the most important question you can answer. Once you've truly answered why your purpose matters, you've hit bedrock, and you can now build with confidence. And you will need this confidence! At various times during the succession planning process, you will be challenged, questioned, and maybe even ridiculed for your attempt. Some members of the organization will raise the old saw, "If it ain't broke don't try to fix it." Others will contend that you don't need a succession planning process in order to pick a successor— "Just make a selection," they bellow, "and let everyone know who will take over when you're no longer here." Some will even say that succession is a problem for the next generation to figure out. I suppose each of these suggestions could be an option, but I would not recommend any of them as a viable approach. With your why in place, you can better address the challenges to your succession plan.

Let me offer an example. I have a terrific client and friend whom I've represented, as well as respected, for many years. He owns a business that started forty years ago as a one-room shop and grew it into the very technical and sophisticated manufacturing company it is today. He has a number of working patents to his name and has grown the company to employ over sixty highly skilled and well-paid employees. Although he has been able to financially secure his retirement quite comfortably, there was no family member or current employee capable of taking the helm after my friend's departure. A few years ago, he began to struggle with thoughts of his succession, and even though he didn't really need any more money, he realized that he did need to find a successor to run the business.

Once I started to work with him, we sat down and discussed how best to proceed. He realized he had accomplished just about everything one could imagine in his business, and now he was looking for a clear reason to go through a succession plan. One option he was actually considering was shutting the business down and simply renting his properties as warehouse space. After several meetings and some serious soul searching, however, my friend hit on his *why* for crafting a succession plan: to ensure his employees' wellbeing!

My client realized that if he did not find an appropriate successor, his employees could be faced with an unsatisfactory new employer; worse, they could lose their jobs. For the client, this thought was untenable. His employees were not just like family to him—they were his family. They weren't blood relations, but they were the family he had created through forty years of shared sweat and tears. His employees invested their lives in the same company he had. These men and women endured the business with him, faced all the same challenges, and celebrated the same successes. Accordingly, my client wanted to bequeath these employees a workplace in which they would be valued and continue to thrive.

This commitment to his employees was the client's why. For the wellbeing of his employees, he wanted to make sure his business successfully transitioned to a new successor. After determining the why, we embarked on a succession plan that involved a two-track process. The first track was to search for a chief operating officer who could come into the business and learn, with the eventual goal of becoming the chief executive officer. The second track of the plan was to engage an investment banker who could fairly value the company and then find an appropriate buyer.

During the yearlong process of travelling both tracks, there were several rather stressful moments for the business owner. In large part, the tension came from his unfamiliarity with the process of hiring a COO, and of working with investment bankers. Wouldn't that cause just about anyone stress? Nevertheless, every time I noticed the owner going off the rails and getting ready to shut the process down, we would review his options. And every time we did this, we returned to his why. Invariably, the business owner agreed that fulfilling his goal was worth navigating the challenges ahead.

I am happy to report that this client achieved success with his succession process, and today he is comforted to know that his employees are in a secure situation. I truly believe if this client had not started with his why, he would have lost focus during the process, and he would never have found such a satisfying solution. As you can see, it is vital that you articulate your own why for undertaking your company's succession plan. Moreover, when you and your team can collectively answer why you want to complete a successful succession, you will gain both personal and collective commitment.

Simon Sinek, in his international best seller *Start with Why*, argues that if more companies began their business planning by answering "why," they would be much more successful. Sinek's book demonstrates that most profitable businesses use this "why" approach to develop new products, introduce new services, and implement new processes. When people and organizations start with why, more people in the organization wake up feeling fulfilled by the work they do.[29] I believe answering the question why is critical for everyone involved in the succession planning process, especially in this purpose stage. Challenging yourself to seek collective answers for this important question of why will give you the energy and drive you need to succeed.

Once you have answered why, please remember to express that answer in writing, for you can seriously jeopardize the entire succession process if your rationale is not recorded. As the Chinese proverb holds, the faintest ink is more powerful than the strongest memory. This does not mean your why is written in stone, but it does mean you will have a much better chance of leading your team and family through the process when your goals are detailed in writing.

There will be times during any project or challenge your company undertakes when stakeholders can become distracted by other matters or become weary of the venture itself. While I make few promises in this book, I can guarantee that there will be times when you or some other important stakeholder will challenge or question your succession planning process.

Bestselling author Ryan Holiday says, "There are far more failures in the world due to a collapse of will than there will ever be from objectively conclusive external events."[30] When you face a challenge, you need a North Star to rely upon and the energy it provides to keep you going. When your team's collective engine is running low or there is a conflict, your why will remind everyone of the reason you are on this succession planning path.

Finally, and before moving forward, once the why has been developed, I suggest you go back and confirm it still squares with your core principles. Hopefully, the why supports and represents your principles, and when it does, you can view this as confirmation that you are on the right path. If the two are in conflict, however, you must ensure that you have the right principles and/or the correct why before you proceed.

What Does Failure Look Like?

Though looking at the positive side of things has always been my preference, considering what failure might look like is just as important. You need to understand the stakes you are playing for in this process. Examining what will happen to your organization if your plan fails may not be something you want to address, but I think it is a crucial exercise.

This practice allows you and the group to be honest with one another. When you describe the results of failure, hopefully the group will gain a greater appreciation for the organization and not think so much about themselves and their personal stake. If your company fails, so will each and every goal of its individual stakeholders.

As the saying goes, the strength in the wolf pack is the wolf but the strength in the wolf is in the pack. Most organizations can overcome great challenges and achieve remarkable results if you work together. It is when one individual thinks he or she is more important than the organization that things begin to fall apart.

While it may seem hard to do, you still need to ask yourself what failure could look like. Ask yourself this series of questions: (i) If I don't proceed with this succession plan, what will happen to the rest of the stakeholders?; (ii) If I don't successfully transfer the business, what is likely to happen to my employees, family, customers and everyone else who depends on me and my business?; and (iii) If I don't proceed, what will happen to my own and my family's legacy?

While I understand that you undertake a succession planning processes to avoid all of these potential failures, I still think it is important to realize, as well as document, potential negative outcomes. Moreover, when you spend time examining the results of failure, it also provides motivation to get it right. In looking at failure, you will better appreciate the need for success!

Purpose
1. What are the Core Principles of Stakeholders? • Integrity • Provide top quality service • Respect employees like customers —everyone is family
2. What is the Ultimate Succession Plan Vision? (Find your North Star) • A new CEO, fully accepted by management and board of directors; ownership, effectively leading the company
3. Why? (Does Vision Align with Core Principles?) • To ensure the continued success of the Company for the shareholders, employees and community
4. What Does Failure Look Like? • No support for next generation of leaders, causing family discord and loss of Company value

Keys to Chapter

1. Establish your values and principles in order to guide you through the succession planning process.

2. After you establish your values and principles, set a vision for your plan. Without a vision, you will not know if your actions are taking you closer to your vison or pulling you further away from it.

3. With your values and vision established, ask yourself why you want to take on this project. The why will establish the foundation for your entire succession plan.

4. As important as it is to know your vision, it is just as important to know what failure looks like. Becoming familiar with failure and how to avoid it will give you the motivation to proceed.

CHAPTER ELEVEN: THE DISCOVERY STAGE

"You first need to determine where you are before you can get to where you want to be."

– Bradley J. Franc

I am not a "mall person", so I don't know my way around our local mall like my wife or daughter does. I could probably blindfold them, and they'd still get to their favorite stores! (I don't mean this to sound gender-specific; in my family it is just a fact.) As soon as I park in the mall's lot, I'm at their mercy: "Where am I going?" I ask. "Do I go left or right at the top of the hill?" It doesn't end there. Once I'm inside, my anxiety only gets worse.

You can imagine that when I visit the mall without their expert guidance, it's not a pretty picture. One day, though, I found a solution to my mall angst—that big map planted near every entrance. Since that discovery, I'm a changed man. When I'm on a solitary mission to buy new shoes, for instance, I find the mall map, look for that big red dot that shows my location, locate the shoe store, and determine the quickest path. This scenario is similar to the key premise of The Succession Solution℠ *Discovery Stage*. If you are to achieve your succession objectives, you must first discover your current position. Once you have located your "red dot" ("You Are Here") in the succession planning mall, you will be ready to chart the path and reach your goals.

In the *Purpose Stage*, you established where you ultimately wanted to arrive—your proverbial shoe store. You then determined why you would want to undertake your succession plan, and then you established a manner for getting there. The next logical step for you, then, is to decide, confirm, and mark that big red dot on your succession planning map. In other words, you need to locate your starting point.

Another reason for locating your position in this process is to ensure that all significant stakeholders are on the same page (or starting from the same dot). As you've seen in earlier chapters, it's not unusual for stakeholders in your company to situate their latitude and longitude lines for your company's succession in fundamentally different spots. This can be the case both in establishing the value of your company and in deciding the qualifications of the next generation of leaders. Thus, it is critical that you and your major stakeholders agree upon your company's current location for the succession planning process.

Before beginning any project, mission, or assignment, it is essential to know where you are in the process. Before a golfer selects a club, he or she needs to know where the ball lies on the hole. We don't use the same club for a ball 400 yards from the hole as we do for one that's only three feet away. If this step is ignored, a whole lot of energy can be exerted only to go the wrong way or miss the mark.

Even though this stage of the succession planning process might seem fundamental or simple—why take time to evaluate where you are, when the answer is so obvious? —I encourage you not to skip it. It is critical that you formally confirm your current situation, because shortcutting or sidestepping this process can jeopardize the entire plan. As Orrin Woodward writes, "There are many shortcuts to failure, but there are no shortcuts to true success." When it comes to succession planning, there is a logical order to follow for success.

Another value the *Discovery Stage* affords is the real possibility that you will uncover something about your company that you did not realize or had forgotten. Persistence at this stage can save you a lot of time, money, and aggravation, especially if you uncover facts, issues, and/or business structures you never realized existed. To ignore this step is to run the risk of having to amend your plan to accommodate some fact about your business structure that you'd forgotten or never knew about in the first place.

Let me share an example to illustrate what I mean. I was once engaged by a very large and successful financial planning firm. The founder realized the importance of succession planning, and he came to me with a proposal to provide equity to his key employees. One of his main concerns, however, was management control. While he wanted to offer equity to key members of his team, he was not yet ready to relinquish complete control. As a result, he suggested we create voting and non-voting control stock for his company. With these two classes of stock, he could transfer almost all of his equity, but still remain in managerial control.

Because I thought we were moving a little too quickly, however, I began to ask some questions about his company. During this inquiry process, I discovered that the business was not a corporation, but rather a limited partnership. As a result, the business owner did not need to create voting and non-voting stock. Rather, he could elect to distribute limited partnership issues without losing management control. As this example demonstrates, a careful review of a business owner's current commercial structure can eliminate a false start.

Only after we'd uncovered the legal structure of his business could we then begin the process of building the owner's succession plan in earnest. Had we started with the assumption that he was a corporation, we would have spent a fair amount of time and money developing one plan, only to be forced to double back and amend that plan once we'd uncovered the firm's basic legal structure.

Although some clients I work with are fully confident that they know exactly where they are with respect to their current ownership and succession plan, many business owners never really give a second thought to their position in this process. Some clients don't recall what legal structures are already in place, and others don't realize that what they have in place can impact the transfer of their business.

Many first-generation business owners, for instance, set up their business in a manner that helps them get started and/or provides additional liability protection, like a corporation or limited liability company. It should come as no surprise that a succession plan was not a high priority when these individuals first formed their company. Survival was the main concern in those early days, which is a natural and reasonable focus. However, time moves more quickly than we realize. When I ask business owners what legal structure or structures they have in place for their succession plan, most of them do not know.

Not having a legal structure that aligns with your succession plan—or not understanding how your legal structure will impact that plan—is like dying without a will. Because so many Americans do die without a will in place, in its absence, each state in our country has laws that provide for the transfer of the deceased's estate. This situation is called "dying intestate." If you die intestate, rest assured the state in which you reside has written a will for you. The sad part about having the state write your will, though, is that the outcome may be completely different from what you had in mind.

In law school, we were taught about the "doctrine of laughing heirs," and it was one of my favorite principles. The doctrine highlights what can happen when you die without a will. Family members whom you never liked (or never even had contact with when you were alive) inherit your estate. The doctrine is named to describe the hilarity of these heirs, who snicker as you are laid to rest, knowing they are the beneficiaries, not of your action, but of your inaction!

Not knowing your current business structure or the ancillary documents that can affect your situation does not mean you are ignorant of their importance, or that you are cavalier about the future of your loved ones. It is common to forget what you may have put in place five, ten, or even twenty-five years ago. However, it does mean that at this point in the succession planning process—the *discovery stage*—you must make sure you examine what's already in place and ascertain how it will impact your plan. You have a busy schedule, and most of you are too busy trying to put out daily fires to focus on the legal or business structure of your succession plan. Thus, after a little digging, you often discover that the existing structure will not achieve your desired results for succession.

A few years ago, I worked with a successful second-generation business owner who operated four separate commercial divisions as sole proprietor. The owner's business provided a service to the restaurant industry, and he had inherited it from his father. With three children, and only one son working in the company, the owner had a specific vision for his succession. He wanted to transfer the business down to his son who was working in the business. However, the father had one exception: if the son sold the business, the proceeds from the sale were to be divided among all three of the father's children.

The specificity of this succession plan demonstrates a great example of a business owner who knew where he wanted to go but did not appreciate the structure required to reach his destination. If the business owner had remained as a sole proprietor, it would have been almost impossible to accomplish his goal. Although a sole proprietorship is a very simple and basic business model, it is a difficult structure to transfer—in fact, it isn't even a legal structure. Further, maintaining his sole proprietorship structure wouldn't provide a way to ensure that his son would divide the sale proceeds among his siblings. Finally, a sole proprietorship offers the least amount of credit protection for the business owner, his family, and/or a potential buyer. In fact, because a sole proprietor business owner is personally liable for any and all actions of the business, I seldom recommend it to clients.

In order to achieve his succession plan, I recommended the owner convert the sole proprietorship into a limited liability company. Afterwards, he could begin transferring the company to his son. In addition, the father could enter into a legal agreement with his son about any subsequent sale to ensure his other children would receive their share of the realized funds.

Where Are We Now?

To improve the likelihood of an effective succession plan, begin by taking an inventory of the existing structure of your business, family, and ownership. Make sure you understand where you are in the mall of succession planning!

Below is a list of items to review during the discovery process:

- Form of business—Corporation, LLC, Partnership
- If a corporation, is it an S-Corp or a C-Corp?
- Ownership interests: who are the owners and how much do they own?
- Are there shareholder agreements in place; what is their impact on your plan?

- Who are the members of your board of directors?
- Who are the officers of the company?
- Who are your key employees?
- Do you have employment agreements with key employees?
- Family dynamics: do you have family members inside the business?
- Financial condition or net worth of the business owner
- Obligation to third parties (banks)
- Important customer and supplier relationships
- Key assets outside of the business (real estate)

Once you review and understand these items, along with any other important matters that may exist for your business, you will want to identify all material items that may impact your succession plan, and list them on the form.

You can retain a summary of all documents, structures, and issues you review, but I recommend you also record them in a separate document or file. Don't try to include everything on The Succession Solution^{SM}, because the goal in this phase is to identify the most significant structural issues impacting your succession plan. The one-page Succession Solution^{SM} system may differ from other planning tools at this point, because it has not been designed to list every single issue that may arise during succession planning—only the material issues. At this stage in the succession planning process, your most effective resolve should be to tackle the *material* issues.

I have witnessed too many plans fail under the sheer weight of a document that lists every minute issue. When presented with a fifteen-page plan—or even longer—I can almost guarantee its failure. Perhaps these lengthy plans work sometimes, but more often than not, they collapse under their own bulk.

Another value or benefit of the *Discovery Stage* is that it displays the plan's structure to all stakeholders engaged in the process. For some stakeholders, the information presented at this stage may be nothing new, but for others, it may be the first time they are presented with certain issues. For instance, for family businesses with more than one shareholder, there is often a shareholder agreement in place that dictates where the stock of a shareholder will go in the event of a death, insolvency, or stock sale. It is vital that all stakeholders understand the impact of these documents; what's more, the shareholders' agreement may be more restrictive than anticipated. When stakeholders become aware of key structural matters, they become better informed and thus more able to discern the solution they desire.

What Succession Planning is Already in Place?

Once you identify and understand all major legal and tax structures, family dynamics, key customers, and/or employee circumstances that can impact your succession plan, you can then determine what (if anything), is currently in place for the succession of your business. In other words, based on what you have learned about your company's existing situation, you can ask yourself these key questions: In the event of the majority shareholder's death, disability, and/or insolvency, what will happen with respect to the succession of my business with the existing structure and agreements in place? What will happen if a major shareholder wants to sell the business?

It is vital to walk through these potential scenarios, even though you may need to consult with your attorney, accountant, and/or financial adviser for insight into what would happen to your business, spouse, children, and employees if you decide to sell the business, become disabled, pass away, or decide to bring on another partner. Don't try to imagine every possible situation, or you will never complete the plan. Reserve your focus for those major events most likely to occur and determine potential outcomes.

Many succession plans fail at this stage of the process, because few business owners realize or appreciate that *how you've structured your personal affairs* can dramatically and fundamentally impact your succession plan. When a succession plan is in conflict with your personal, legal, or financial situation, it's in trouble.

Many situations in your personal life can impact your succession plan. To avoid potential conflicts, you must investigate your personal business affairs to see if they are in harmony with your succession vision. For example, have you personally guaranteed any of the company's debt, or the debt of any other business? If so, a lender may have a claim on your stock when you try to sell or transfer it, or if you die while owning the stock. Will your spouse need the income earned from your business to support the current standard of living? And if you want an heir to take over your business, have you considered how you will manage the personal needs of your spouse?

How your estate plan is structured is fundamental to your succession plan. Do you have a will in place, and does it address the transfer of your business? Do you have a power of attorney in the event you become incapacitated due to an accident or illness? Many people don't realize that if you become disabled by an accident or illness, your business can be placed in a perilous situation. If you become debilitated without a power of attorney in place, no one can act on behalf of you without court involvement, and obtaining judicial approval can be very time consuming and expensive.

Early in my legal career, I was asked to assist a young woman whose husband had a successful sign company. Unfortunately, during one of the sign installation projects, the husband fell off his ladder-truck. He was badly hurt and fell into a coma for weeks. Like many startup companies, the husband had formed a corporation whereby he was the sole owner. He was also the president, secretary, treasurer, and sole director of the board. In other words, and like so many other small businesses, he was everything. His wife told me the business was profitable and had a number of loyal employees willing to help her in this difficult time. However, she had no idea how she could continue to run the business without help.

There was no power of attorney in place for the husband, which meant the wife could not sign anything for the company. Payroll checks could not be issued; banks and vendors could not be paid. The operations of the business came to a halt. The owner's wife was placed in an awful situation. She had to witness the failure of her husband's business because there was no document authorizing her to act on his behalf! Her husband eventually came out of his coma and recovered some of his normal activities, but because no one could act in his place while he was incapacitated, the business was lost.

Had the husband granted his wife a power of attorney prior to his accident, she could have acted on her husband's behalf and saved the business. She would have been legally permitted to perform any business matter or transaction. She could have ensured that the bank and the employees were paid. Instead, the business shut down and caused significant financial hardship to the owner, his wife, and the employees whose livelihoods relied on the sign company.

Another often overlooked personal matter that can impact the successful transition of a business involves debt. Practically all businesses I have worked with borrow money. Borrowing money is a very effective way to manage your cash-flow. In fact, in a fast-growing business, borrowing money is almost required. As your company grows, it must meet weekly or bi-weekly payroll demands. However, your customers may be paying invoices in thirty, sixty, or ninety-day increments, which can cause a real strain on cash flow. As a result, you might obtain a line of credit to finance account receivables and satisfy immediate cash demands.

In most lending or financing arrangements, such as a line of credit or term loan, it is common for loan documents to contain "events of default," which would cause the loan to default, giving the lender or bank certain rights to take possession of collateral or even your business. One typical event of default contained in most loan documents occurs upon the passing of the majority shareholder. As stated, many business owners do not realize this provision is contained within their bank documents. I have seen a number of businesses fail (or nearly fail) because the bank demanded payment in full upon the owner's passing. I once worked with a very successful business owner whose largest business holding was in the retail industry. This client had identified a relative as the successor of his business. The acknowledged successor had spent his entire adult life preparing to take over for the business owner, and everyone was in agreement about his succession.

The business owner had many other business assets, from significant commercial real estate holdings to investments in the food industry. In fact, at the time of his passing, he owned over seventy different business interests. Some were wildly successful, while others were insolvent. Almost all business interests held by the business owner were unrelated to his main retail business. Further, as part of his real estate holdings, there was significant bank financing on many of the properties.

Prior to his death, I explained the significant death taxes the business owner would incur at his passing, as well as the possibility that the banks holding his debt may demand payment at the same time. He thanked me for my comments, but assured me he had enough liquidity and equity in his real estate holdings to guarantee the banks would continue to carry the loans even at his passing.

The business owner passed away in 2008, and as many may recall, this was at the depth of the great recession. As everything this business owner held dropped in value, his commercial real estate holdings collapsed. At the same time, of course, the banks were under severe pressure to ensure their loans were in good standing. Bank regulators viewed events of default very unfavorably. The business owner's death could not have come at a more inopportune time.

If not for the hard work of his successor, the business owner's entire estate and businesses could have been lost. Hard decisions had to be made. The main retail business was forced to liquidate many assets to satisfy the banks. In the end, the business owner's succession plan was hindered due to issues that were only peripherally related to the main business.

Final Thoughts on Discovery

The examples offered above provide pertinent case studies of why it is crucial for you to understand where you stand both legally and structurally before starting the succession planning process. The very act of going through this process allows you to gain valuable insight into the safeguards that must be put in place for succession when and if something happens to you.

Part of this process may also involve determining who's responsible for paying certain costs associated with the transfer of your business (whether by death or otherwise). It is always important to understand the tax liability involved in any succession plan and who will bear the cost. For instance, should your business bear the cost or a particular beneficiary? Regardless, it is important to make sure the cost of succession is properly allocated to the person you think should incur those costs or taxes.

Additionally, how assets are titled or how beneficiary designation language is defined will often control how assets can be transferred. The title to assets or the beneficiary designation of a significant asset can dramatically impact your business's succession plan. Each state has its own laws as to how it treats the title to certain assets. For most states, property held between husband and wife will automatically transfer to the survivor. As a result, if you provide in your will that the ownership of your company will go to a particular person, your plans may be upset if ownership is held jointly between you and your spouse.

I was recently assisting a third-generation owner with his company's succession plan. When I asked him to show me his company's by-laws, he was surprised by the request. He told me there was nothing in the by-laws that would address any transition of his business to the next generation. To the business owner's surprise, I discovered an old amendment that restricted the transfer of stock, which would have put his current succession plan in violation of the by-laws. He told me he had completely forgotten about that amendment and stated it no longer applied. Unfortunately, until a formal amendment to the provision was agreed upon among all parties, the old amendment was still enforceable. We ended up amending the by-laws. I share this story to show how crucial it is to understand the business and legal structures already in place at this stage of the succession planning process.

While the first step in the *Discovery Stage* is designed to uncover where your business stands with respect to structure and ownership, the next step discloses what is already in place for succession, even if your business has forgotten about such provisions. You can engage the assistance of your CPA and attorney in reviewing what you have in place for succession. They can review your existing business records and let you know what will happen and who will be in charge of your process. You don't need to understand and commit to memory every last detail, but it is important to have a firm understanding of the current structures in place that might impact your business's new succession plan.

Once you have a basic understanding of where you are and what is in place with respect to your business, you can then move on to the next stage of determining where you want to go and why. For this reason, it is critical to complete both sections in the *Discovery Stage* before moving to the *Challenge Stage*. List the top four to five most important elements that describe your current situation, and then list the documents or other items currently in place that will dictate the progression of your succession plan.

Discovery

5. **Where are we now and what is in place for succession?**

   (Where is the Red Dot?)

   (Management, Ownership, Employees, Family Dynamics)

   - Shareholders' Agreement in place
   - Management correctly in place
   - No plan for next CEO

Keys to Chapter

1. Before you can proceed with your succession plan, take stock of any structures or provisions that may already be in place.

2. Not having a succession plan is like dying without a will: the state where you reside will decide for you. It is important to know what you have in place and what state law will dictate.

3. During the process, you will likely discover issues you did not fully understand or had forgotten. Identifying them at this stage will allow you to better plan for succession.

CHAPTER TWELVE: THE CHALLENGE STAGE

"Your moment of maximum risk is also your moment of maximum opportunity."

– Adrian J. Slywaotzky

While each stage in The Succession Solution℠ is important, the *Challenge Stage* may uncover the greatest opportunities for a successful transition. This is the stage where you not only identify the strengths and opportunities of undertaking your business's succession plan, but also confront potential obstacles.

As international business consultant Adrian Slywaotzky points out, your business's greatest opportunities are often found by examining its greatest risks. Slywaotzky states that businesses often focus too much on opportunities and don't leave enough time, resources, or energy to consider threats. If a significant threat arises, your opportunities can be threatened. As a result, to improve the chances of success, you need to focus on all three elements—strengths, opportunities, and obstacles. We'll discuss later on how you can then begin to look for ways to eliminate or mitigate the risk.

In essence, completing the *Challenge Stage* of The Succession Solution℠ solidifies the foundation of your succession plan. Before you construct both your three-year and one-year plans, you will need to actively examine each element presented in the *Challenge Stage* as it relates to your plan's strengths, opportunities, and obstacles.

This stage is critical to your succession planning process. You cannot develop and implement your long-and short-term goals without it. In fact, if you don't identify potential threats to your plan, you risk being blindsided and could end up sacrificing the precious time needed to transform or overcome these threats. Generating goals for your succession plan without confronting the latent threats uncovered by working through the *Challenge Stage* will greatly diminish your chances of success.

The *Challenge Stage* is designed like a standard SWOT analysis. SWOT is an acronym for Strengths, Weaknesses, Opportunities, and Threats, and it depicts an analytical process many organizations perform as part of their strategic planning process. SWOT analyses provide you with a clear assessment of your company's overall health by producing a straightforward snapshot of its strengths and weaknesses. Once completed, management often refers back to its SWOT to ensure that each of the identified weaknesses or threats has been addressed.

It is commonplace for sports teams to use a SWOT analysis before taking on an opponent, for only after identifying their strengths and weaknesses, and understanding their opportunities, can a game plan be developed. Similarly, before you take on the challenge of finalizing your specific succession plan, you need to perform your own SWOT analysis. Remember, however, that while your SWOT analysis is similar to that of a coach or player, the stakes are often much higher in business.

Instead of the conventional SWOT format, I use a slightly modified approach in The Succession Solution℠. Threats and weaknesses are often the same, so I focus on strengths, opportunities, and obstacles only. In the succession planning process, a weakness that is not also a threat isn't worth your attention, so I've eliminated this unnecessary step.

Like a winning coach, you will rely on your succession planning team to assist you in accomplishing your overall goals. Utilize the diverse insights of your team at this stage as you work collaboratively to identify the strengths, opportunities, and obstacles your succession process might present for your organization. Using this modified SWOT process is sure to bring fresh ideas as you work together to understand the potential threats and dangers your company may face when planning for succession.

During the *Challenge Stage*, encourage your team members to express their ideas fully, and invite any and all perspectives. Record their insights and viewpoints on a white board or write them on poster-sized paper and hang them around the room to invite ongoing reflection and fine-tuning. Encourage participants to discuss each view and idea raised, and then work as quickly as possible to arrive at a consensus—which should also be recorded.

Strengths

Strengths refer to your company's ability to accomplish tasks. Your strengths are the bulwarks of your business, and they can take many forms. Some examples of strengths that will fortify your succession plan are a strong financial position, a commitment to taking the time to complete your plan, having key employees, and trusting your assembled team. Strengths can exist in a recognizable brand name and in your company's reputation. I advocate starting with your company's strengths, because too many business owners forget or ignore them, and this can be a costly oversight. When you recognize and honor the strengths inherent in your organization as assets, you can use these assets to support and confirm the succession planning process.

As you work to identify strengths, look at both tangible and intangible assets. Pinpoint the resources your organization possesses that can help you mitigate, avoid, and/or exploit any of the risks you identified earlier in the planning process. Detecting your strengths is crucial, because you will use these assets to help you through the rough patches of the succession planning process.

Again, a sports analogy illustrates how you can play to your strengths. When an NFL team has a great quarterback but an inferior running game, a smart coach isn't going to rely on the running game to win. Rather, this coach will trust the quarterback to score. Of course, no coach wants to be dependent on the quarterback to make every play, but he should be used as a primary asset. Similarly, when working through a succession plan, every organization has a number of resources available, and you and your team will want to utilize these strengths during periods of transition. For instance, a company with a strong balance sheet may be able to withstand the fluctuations caused by the unexpected passing of a CEO or majority owner. A family with strong relationships built on trust can draw upon this asset to weather the storms of transition.

Once identified, your organization's strengths should be clearly articulated to the whole team. These are the qualities that will help ease the panic and anxiety often associated with an unexpected change. Moreover, you'll need to draw upon these assets to tackle your succession risks, so it is important to list and prioritize them. Remember that some of these resources may be more important than others. At this stage, I suggest listing your top three to five strengths—those that could have the greatest impact on your succession plan. For instance, while it's clearly a plus to have favorable lease terms for your office, it would probably be more important to have a strong balance sheet to help withstand the challenges resulting from naming a new leadership team.

Opportunities

After you have identified and prioritized the strengths you will draw upon to accomplish your company's succession plan, begin a similar process to identify your opportunities. In succession planning, opportunities refer to any matters that you and your team are excited about, like developing new skills, generating company-wide optimism for the future, or increasing customer security.

Opportunities can (and often do) include resolving and overcoming any current threats and dangers within your organization and the succession plan. In this case, opportunities are the beneficial outcomes that are made possible by eliminating an existing threat or danger. For instance, when a shareholder who has so far been resistant to succession planning suddenly decides to come on board, it can energize your entire team.

In this phase of the *Challenge Stage*, you and your team will want to identify every opportunity you can imagine. To avoid being overwhelmed, prioritize by itemizing the top three to five opportunities you want to exploit. It is crucial to remember that the *general* definition of an opportunity is a set of circumstances that makes something else possible, but also understand that in a *business* situation, this definition is more targeted and specific. Business opportunities should be exciting and worthwhile, but you must understand that such prospects do not come without risk, and they usually require the use of additional resources.

For instance, you may have a goal to find a new CEO with all the attributes of a Fortune 500 leader, but if your organization does not have the resources to hire such a person, taking such a financial risk will be the wrong opportunity to pursue at this time. Obviously, finding and hiring a new CEO in the next three to five years will be impacted by the resources you are willing and able to dedicate to that position.

On the other hand, some opportunities have a clear and present advantage, and should be seized upon immediately. For example, the successful transfer of management to the next generation of family members may provide renewed employee confidence, because workers know your company will succeed beyond the next generation. Another opportunity could rest in the confidence your customers, vendors, and/or lenders will gain by learning you have a transition plan. Still another may be your ability to spend more time with your family or pursue other outside interests once a succession plan is in place.

Clearly, the *Challenge Stage* of the succession process is both vital and complex. While it is important for you to identify your opportunities, you must understand that pursuing these prospects will require both resources and risk. Accordingly, only after reviewing all three parts of this stage (Strengths, Opportunities, and Threats), can you and your team better assess whether you can or even want to pursue a given opportunity. Once this phase of the *Challenge Stage* has been completed, you will know which opportunities to execute, and the prospects selected will provide the platform for creating your long-term and short-term succession planning goals.

Obstacles

Just as the *Challenge Stage* is one of the most important stages in The Succession Solution^{SM} process, identifying obstacles or threats is one of the most important phases in the *Challenge Stage*. In the obstacle phase, you must identify major obstacles and pinpoint potential dangers blocking the achievement of your succession plan. For instance, if you are not successful in transferring your business to the next generation, it could result in a loss of your business or a key employee, and this is a potential danger.

A few years ago, I was asked to work with a third-generation regional building supply company started decades earlier by two brothers. While the business had enjoyed three generations of success, by the time I came onboard, it was experiencing new challenges. In the past, the organization had supplied materials to many homebuilders in the area. Due to the recent entry of large national track home builders into the market, however, many local contractors— representing the building supply company's main customers—were forced out of business. As the national track builder's business expanded, fewer independent construction companies could compete, and as a result, the building supply company's business began to stall.

Adding to the stress of the company's survival was the fact that, by the third generation, the company had over fifteen shareholders living all over the world. This large and diverse shareholder group was the result of passing stock ownership down to the various children of the two original founders. At this point in time, however, only four shareholders worked in the business, and relied on it for their livelihood.

As with many companies possessing both inside and outside shareholders, the inside shareholders (those working in the business) were in a dogfight for survival—they needed every dollar in the company to compete and find new markets. However, the outside shareholders believed they should be receiving a return on their investment (dividends), just as their parents had for so many years.

The inside shareholders met with me in an attempt to figure out a fair solution to their situation. Both groups of shareholders felt strongly about their positions. Adding even more of a challenge to this scenario was the fact that the four inside shareholders held unequal ownership of the company, and, of course, they did not agree on a possible solution. Family discord was running rampant, not only between the inside and outside shareholders, but among the insiders as well.

The inside shareholders told me that despite being well aware of the importance of succession planning for the company's continuation, they had not been able to make any real progress with their succession solution. In fact, they had worked for nearly ten years with their prior law firm, achieving little to no progress.

After reviewing three generations of legal documents and paperwork (which felt like translating the Dead Sea Scrolls!), I again met with the four inside shareholders. We spent the first part of the day carefully interpreting what their existing documents, agreements, and trust provided. Once we understood what was currently in place, we moved on to look at the risks they were facing as a result of their inaction. The afternoon was spent examining the outcomes and risks associated with taking no further action, and there were many very real perils on the horizon: losing their jobs, their investments, the forfeiture of community jobs, and ultimately, the loss of their grandparents' legacy. After studying each of these risks, the four inside shareholders began to find common ground. They began to recognize that, while it may not be possible for each individual shareholder to accomplish 100 percent of his or her goal, compromise would be preferable to losing the company.

Our next step was to explain the obstacles to the outside shareholders. In particular, we wanted to make sure they understood the risks associated with taking no action. Hoping to uncover any other hazards we may have missed, we then opened the process to all shareholders. During this larger meeting, the outside shareholders quickly realized that the insiders were truly concerned about the company's survival. They weren't just focused on how much money they could "take out" of the company. This recognition was a game changer.

After meeting with the entire shareholder group, we developed an eight-step plan for succession. Each step of the process addressed the risks individual shareholders had identified in a descending order of priority. What's more, I explained to the inside shareholders that if we accomplished even four of the eight steps, we will have accomplished a victory.

I am pleased to report that after three years of hard work, we completed all eight steps, and the company continues to survive, even with the continued presence of the national home builders. We have now begun a succession plan for the next generation of owners. We are exploring the benefits of an employee stock ownership plan, because there are no family members who are interested in working in the business.

The fulfillment of this building supply company's succession plan validates the significance of working through the *Challenge Stage* of The Succession Solution℠. Not only does this stage help you identify the strengths, opportunities, and obstacles you must navigate during your succession planning process, it shows how these factors can be used to benefit the plan itself.

By identifying the obstacles and/or risks your company faces, you will be better prepared to avoid, mitigate, or find an opportunity within these liabilities. The *Challenge Stage* is also a key building block to developing your three-to-one-year goals as you progress through the succession plan. In fact, if you complete only one stage of The Succession Solution℠ process (and, of course, this is not advised), I would recommend it be the *Challenge Stage*.

I really do not know how succession planners could develop long and short-term goals without identifying and addressing possible obstacles to their plans. As a business owner, you must know how to compete in the marketplace, which means you must understand your competition. Similarly, you must understand the roadblocks that can arise as you move forward with succession planning. Only by identifying, confronting, and taking active steps to overcome these obstacles will you be able to make real progress with your succession plan. Andy Grove, former CEO of Intel, says, "Bad companies are destroyed by crisis. Good companies survive them. Great companies are improved by them."[31]

Examples of Succession Obstacles to Consider

Because each and every company has its own distinctive risks, you must spend time identifying the liabilities unique to your succession plans. However, the majority of risks fall within six types, some of which have been previously mentioned. If you and your team discuss and work through the itemized list below, you will dramatically increase your chances of a successful succession.

1. Family Discord

The first succession risk is intra-family discord. As mentioned, statistics show that 60 percent of all family businesses fail to survive to the next generation due to intra-family conflict. Too often, a business fails because family members allow their personal dislike for one another to cloud their professional judgment. I refer to this phenomenon as the "he is touching me syndrome."

I grew up with five other siblings, and often when we took a family vacation, we traveled by station wagon. As I tell my own kids, back then we didn't have smartphones or air conditioning, and we had to listen to the music our parents liked and could find on the limited radio stations. What's more, unlike today's kids in their minivans or SUVs, we didn't have the room to spread out. As a result, after being in a car for hours, it seemed only natural for my brothers and sisters to annoy one another.

Of course, when a fight broke out, my mother or father would apply certain forms of discipline (something modern parents might be discouraged from doing). After a scolding, we were told to keep to ourselves, and not to talk or engage one another. Predictably, a sibling's next great move would be to touch and thus try to annoy another. Writing about this still brings a smile to my immature face.

Sadly, such childish tricks are not limited to youngsters. Competition among family members can last well into adulthood, and disharmony in a family business can be much more damaging than childhood antics. When such competition arises between siblings, parents of siblings, and spouses of siblings, it can be disastrous.

Competition is often advantageous in a business setting, and you might even look for this trait in the candidates you evaluate to hire. However, when competition becomes too intense, or if it is not properly managed, it can become destructive. Particularly in a family business, the impact of sibling rivalry can be especially difficult for parents who must select one offspring over another to be the company's next CEO.

In addition to competition, your inability to interact personably with your family outside the company can create problems. I witnessed a family in-law member who was not selected as the next CEO—despite his obvious skill and experience in running the company—due to his inability to get along with one of the majority owner's spouses who never even worked in the business. You never know where conflict will arise.

2. Unprepared Successor

The second succession difficulty you may encounter is the unpreparedness of the next generation. Research shows a business fails due to the incompetence or ineffectiveness of the next generation nearly 25 percent of the time.[32]

Determining proper preparation can be a hard conversation to have, for it is never easy to provide constructive criticism to a fellow employee. It is even more difficult when you have to confront a family member about his or her incompetence. However, if you don't have this uncomfortable conversation, the pain of a failed company will be greater.

Surprisingly, statistics show that these two risks—intra-family discord and ill-prepared successors—comprise 85 percent of all family business succession failures.[33] If you spend the time to carefully examine these two succession-planning risks, you will dramatically increase your business's chance of survival.

No doubt you would be very happy if I could show you how to improve your company's survival rate by 85 percent. I learned a valuable exercise a number of years ago about solving 80 percent of any problem. If you solve 80 percent of the problem, then return a month or a year later to attack the remaining 20 percent, you will achieve over 90 percent completion. Too many people try to reach a 100-percent solution and fail. As the saying goes, "Don't let perfect be the enemy of good!"

3. Refusal to Cede Control

The third serious risk to succession is the current generation's refusal to cede control or authority. This happens when a senior family member refuses to step away, even when the next generation is ready to assume control, or the senior member is no longer active in the business. At this juncture, it is important to note the contrast between control of ownership and control of management.

As you can imagine, it is challenging to plan for business succession when you are worried that it may involve giving up control. This decision is both vitally important and extremely difficult. However, just because a subject is hard to raise and discuss does not mean it should be excluded from the succession planning process. I have found a third-party facilitator to be invaluable in these stalemate situations. A mediator can raise this matter when the next generation finds itself paralyzed by discomfort.

Another key reason for raising issues of control rests in the fact that a lack of information often surrounds the subject. As mentioned earlier, change in management is different from change in ownership. It is possible for you to remain the majority or sole shareholder while still transferring management to the next generation. In fact, you can transfer nearly all stock and/or ownership interest in the company and still control the ownership.

I recently worked with a business owner on his succession plan. Interestingly, I'd met with this business owner about ten years prior, and at that time, his wife refused to have any discussion about succession. At the time, the owner and his wife both felt the next generation was unprepared to run the business. They now believed the next generation leader was ready to take on the company's daily activities and become the CEO. However, the founders still did not want to give up ultimate control of the business. "What if the next generation wanted to do something completely unacceptable?" they asked.

I explained to my client that if he wanted to transfer stock ownership as well as management to his son, we could transfer ninety-nine percent of the company and still remain in control. By creating voting and non-voting stock, we would issue the founder ninety-nine shares of non-voting stock for each share of voting stock. Afterwards, he could transfer ninety-nine percent of the company to his son and still have 100 percent of the voting control. No one had ever explained this technique to the founder. This business owner, and more importantly his wife, immediately embraced the idea of transferring the non-voting stock to the CEO son. The son was also satisfied, for two important reasons. First, he knew the future value of the company would accrue to him. Second, the father and son entered into an agreement where the son had an option to buy voting control should his father want to sell his shares or in the event of his father's passing.

4. Estate Plan Not Aligned with Succession Plan

The fourth succession risk occurs when your estate plan is not aligned with your company's succession plan. This threat arises when your estate plan bequeaths the ownership or control of the business to a person you did not intend and who does not have the business acumen necessary to make the correct decisions.

For instance, you may designate a family member as the successor of your business. However, if your will directs ownership of stock or equity in your company to your spouse, or to a trust controlled by your spouse, or to someone other than the identified successor, everyone may be in for a big surprise at your passing.

I am not suggesting you leave the equity of your business to your identified successor. Rather, I am proposing that you fully understand the impact of your estate plan on your business's succession. Too many clients I have worked with over the years have not recognized the impact their estate plan can have on their businesses. For example, I met recently with a business client who, many years ago, had named his two adult sons as the beneficiaries of the equity in his business. Regrettably, after the preparation of this client's last estate plan, one of the sons developed a severe substance abuse problem and was incapable of managing his own affairs, let alone making business decisions. Had the business owner passed away prior to amending his estate plan, I am convinced the business would have been lost. Luckily, we were able to amend the estate plan to assign control to the other son, while establishing a trust to protect the son with the substance abuse issue.

5. Failure to Act

The fifth succession risk is the threat of non-action. Taking no action can have an almost narcotic effect. You may feel comfortable with the status quo. You might enjoy the current situation and fear the potential shake up of initiating a succession planning process. However, like many drugs, inaction can become habit forming, and, ultimately, it can become as fatal to your business as addiction is to the life of the addict.

A few years ago I worked with a client who had a terrific sporting equipment business. There were two sons, both active in the business, and both had been gifted stock in the company by their parents. The business was profitable, but the two sons—while both competent—did not work well together. The founder couldn't envision leaving equal interest to his sons as a viable succession plan for the business. When I asked the business owner about his succession plans, he merely stated that he didn't know what he was going to do. He assumed he'd continue to work and try to figure it out later. Fortunately, I could see something that the business owner could not. It seemed clear to me that he wasn't taking action because he wasn't wholly aware of his options. He had succumbed to the paralysis of putting off this crucial process.

We decided to work through The Succession Solution℠. We spent time working on his goals, concerns, and fears. We then discussed a number of options, from doing nothing, to transferring his business to the next generation, to selling his company to a third party. After we carefully walked through all practical options available, the father felt that, while either son may have been able to run the business on his own, the business would likely fail due to their inability to work together. Therefore, the father's goal was to leave one son the business, but still try to equalize his estate to his two sons. The father decided to transfer the business to his one son, provided that he would agree to purchase his brother's value of the stock. The father wanted to determine the commitment of the son he had selected, and whether or not the other son was interested in selling his interest.

The son who had the option to own the entire business was not forced to buy out his brother's shares. Rather, if he wanted to eventually control and own the entire business, he had to agree to buy his brother's shares. This was a situation where the father gave his son the option, but not the obligation, to take over the business. Feeling confident he could take over the business, the son agreed to the terms. A few years later, when the father passed away, the son who had previously purchased his brother's stock, gladly purchased the remaining stock from his mother, executing a complete buy-out of the company. Thanks to the patriarch's planning and foresight, the company is prospering.

In a 1954 speech, U.S. President Dwight D. Eisenhower quoted a former college president's formulation: "I have two kinds of problems, the urgent and the important. The urgent are not important, and the important are never urgent."[34] This "Eisenhower Principle" is said to be how he organized his workload and priorities. Because your succession plan is not screaming and shouting for immediate attention, the call goes unanswered. Too many times I hear the words, "I know I have to take care of my succession plan, and I will, as soon as I find the time." The reality is that your plan will not be achieved unless you make the time and commit to the process. Instead, someone else's plan will be imposed, and I only hope it is the right one.

6. Death Taxes and Liquidity

The sixth succession risk is associated with death taxes and liquidity. While this risk is very real and must be addressed, there is a reason I placed it sixth on the list. Too many times, the hired CPA or estate planning attorney will use various charts and tables to explain to you all of the taxes to be paid by your estate. This tax or legal professional will then show you techniques and transactions that will produce enormous savings for your estate, and this is an important step in the estate-planning process. However, I have found that many business owners worry so much about estate taxes that they don't focus on the more immediate, life-threating risks their businesses can face. In fact, most businesses I have worked with have been able to endure the death taxes levied at the founder or significant owner's death; failure comes from other oversights.

Your business is often your most significant asset, yet despite its value, most companies are not very liquid. In most cases, you will use your available cash-flow for the payment of creditors, salaries, or capital investments. Thus, when the federal or state government levies a death tax, that liability can be a heavy toll for your business. To exacerbate this situation, these taxes are based on the fair market value of your business, and government agencies do not care whether your company has the liquidity to pay the tax or not. The IRS and most states want to be paid within nine months of a business owner's death. In some instances, the IRS will allow death taxes to be paid over time, but an interest rate is still imposed during this extended pay period.

As you can imagine, death taxes can place an enormous burden on your business, which is why it is so important to understand the risk. However, unlike many of the other risks we've identified, one positive dimension of the risks related to death taxes and liquidity is the ability to quantify them. Death taxes are a risk you can actually calculate with a certain level of accuracy, and once you quantify the risk, you can then decide how you will address it. For instance, you could begin a gifting program to transfer a portion of your equity to the next generation to save on death taxes. You could sell some stock during your life to increase your liquidity. You can buy insurance to fund some of the potential death taxes. There are always options to consider.

Besides the tax liability associated with your death, liquidity risks can also occur with your lender(s). This risk is overlooked far too often in the succession planning process. Most businesses have credit facilities (loans) in place. You may have a line of credit to finance the business's accounts receivable, or you may have loans for capital improvements. Almost every loan I have reviewed for business owners includes an event of default clause that activates on the occasion of an owner's death. This means that, even if you've been current on your loan for years and have a strong balance sheet, the event of your passing will place that loan in default.

I have discussed this issue with many lenders, and they tell me this practice is simply part of their underwriting process. They know the statistics associated with the transfer of a business to the next generation, and they don't want to assume the risk. So, instead, they shift the risk onto the business. Thus, at probably the worst time in the life of your business, it becomes the most financially vulnerable. This is why I advise that all business owners who are undertaking a succession plan speak to their lender(s) about liquidity risks to see how best to mitigate or eliminate them.

Obviously, as an owner, you want to assess and control the risks associated with your business. The succession planning process is handled in the same manner. Even if you cannot get a lender to eliminate the event of default clause, it is still important to acknowledge this risk and discuss it with your team. Even though most lenders will not remove the provision, by meeting with a lender soon after the passing of the founder or significant owners, you are more likely to work out a plan than if you ignore it. Confronting such risks is always preferable to receiving an unexpected event of default notice.

Another significant risk is having to reassure key customers of yours who are concerned that your company will not survive the passing of the founder or key executive. This can prove a fatal risk for your company, especially if you have a significant concentration of your business with a concerned customer. Your client's primary concern is his or her own wellbeing in the event of your succession or passing.

A number of years ago, I was engaged by a large construction company to assist with its succession plan in response to the demands of its bonding company. The contractor's bonding company realized that if the CEO/founder passed away unexpectedly, the company's current project(s) would be at risk. Consequently, if projects were at risk, the company's bond would be at risk also. It sounded to me like the bonding company was performing its own SWOT analysis on its clients! Clearly, this contractor's succession planning process needed to consider how its bonds would be satisfied in the event of his (or a future owner's) passing.

The owner's wife worked in the business along with their young son, who would eventually become the future CEO. However, the son had only recently graduated from high school and was not yet prepared for a leadership role. Fortunately, the business had an excellent project manager willing to take on the task. We drafted an agreement that provided a performance bonus to the project manager once he successfully completed the bonded projects. The bonding company found this plan acceptable.

Unfortunately, about two years later, the business owner unexpectedly passed away. However, because the project manager successfully completed the bonded projects, the company survived, and the project manager was generously rewarded.

Focus on What You Can Control

As you identify the obstacles associated with completing your succession plan, be sure to focus only on those obstacles you can control. There is no need to waste time worrying over potential obstacles outside your control. Instead, when you assess which risks to mitigate or to overcome, prioritize only those threats which can be impacted within the next twelve to thirty-six months.

Business owners thrive on exploring opportunities, but they do not focus enough attention on threats. Of course, it is important to capitalize on opportunities, but threats can bring your business to its knees. I firmly believe that the opportunity for a strong succession plan lies in uncovering potential threats and identifying the strengths available to you to confront them.

Once the top three to five obstacles are identified, you and your team can better develop strategies for overcoming them. In fact, after this step is completed, you can review and/or revise the opportunities identified earlier to confirm that they remain your top opportunities to pursue. Once you have listed your company's strengths, opportunities, and obstacles, and have devised strategies for overcoming those obstacles, you are now ready to move forward to the *Mission Stage*.

Challenge

6. Strengths

- Financially strong
- Name recognition in industry
- Good relationship with key customers

7. Opportunities

- Time to decide on next CEO
- New CEO could begin to develop new customer relationships

8. Obstacles

- Family discord on who should be next CEO
- Key customers have close relationship with current CEO

9. Strategies for Overcoming Obstacles

- Have management explain to family CEO recommendations
- Have family member explain who and why they want this CEO
- Have existing CEO begin to introduce next CEO to key customers

Keys to Chapter

1. To improve the chances of success, focus on all three elements during this stage—strength, opportunities, and obstacles

2. As international business consultant Adrian Slywaotzky points out, "Your business's greatest opportunities are often found by examining your greatest risks."

3. Once you identify your strengths, opportunities, and obstacles, then you can proceed in developing your strategies for reaching your long-term goals and vision.

CHAPTER THIRTEEN: THE MISSION STAGE

"Most people overestimate what they can do in one year and underestimate what they can do in ten years."

– Bill Gates

In combat, before any fighting begins, a wise commander will define his mission. The commander will set forth specific tasks to be carried out to achieve the mission's overall goals, and specific tasks are assigned to particular individuals or groups. It is often vital for a mission's tasks to be sequenced in a certain manner. If designated steps or duties are not completed in the right order, the mission is at risk. Thus, the way in which particular tasks are set, and the order in which those tasks are completed, is central to the mission's success.

Operation Desert Storm is a perfect example of a well-defined and precisely executed military mission. The battle plan for attacking and removing the Iraqi army from Kuwait mapped out by General H. Norman Schwarzkopf was one of the most impressive military campaigns ever devised:

> [Schwarzkopf's] mission was to "decapitate" the Iraqi high command by cutting communication links, destroying key government ministries, and leveling places of refuge for Iraq's civilian and military leadership. Attacks on Iraq's command and control network continued throughout the air campaign. Simultaneously, Iraq's airfields and air defense networks were targeted— in order to deny the enemy an opportunity to challenge the allied aerial onslaught. As a result, Iraq's air force was never a factor in the war, and allied warplanes operated with impunity from the Turkish border to southern Kuwait.[35]

Importantly, Schwarzkopf did not just march into Iraq and start fighting—his plan was thoughtful and deliberate. His first step was to deploy military assets in the region. He knew the Iraq military was one of the largest armies in the world, so he could not afford to go in unprepared or undermanned. The first step of the general's mission was to build up a mass of forces and weapons that hadn't been seen in a generation. Step two was initiating the campaign with an overwhelming airstrike. Only after the resources had been accumulated and the air campaign had been accomplished did Schwarzkopf then deliver his so-called left hook by mounting a military attack from the west to surprise the Iraqi army (whose leaders had expected Schwarzkopf to come up from the south). Most military experts predicted the war would last months, but it was over in days and with limited casualties. How was this mission accomplished so smoothly? Through efficient planning!

In stunning contrast, business and government leaders throughout our nation's history have lost their jobs or reelections because of their failure to articulate and execute a clearly-defined mission in the face of great challenge. Whether military, social, or economic, without a well-defined mission, leaders are unable to secure the support and confidence of their teams, and failure to secure confidence can seriously undermine any mission.

Like a good commander preparing for a conflict, you undertake an important mission when you plan for your company's succession. You are the general at the helm of your succession mission, and you must have in place not only a well-defined plan broken into a sequence of steps, but the assets and resources necessary to complete that plan. You will need to execute the plan while simultaneously adjusting to challenges that emerge along the way.

Moving too quickly to achieve your succession plan can also cause frustration. A lack of instant success when deploying a plan may persuade even the staunchest business owner to give up. As a business owner, it is your job to model thoughtful, deliberate, and sequenced planning. When company members witness you rushing to change the organization, only to give up when confronting the first real obstacles, your whole team suffers. Such miscalculations can be avoided by using

The Succession Solution℠ to assist you in developing your mission. You will define the mission of your succession plan by outlining the goals, actions, and measurements of success that must be completed to achieve your plan's purpose, and by confronting your plan's potential obstacles.

While the *Purpose Stage* of The Succession Solution℠ explains why you want to achieve your succession plan, the *Mission Stage* is where you decide what specific actions to take— it is the *how*. In this phase of The Succession Solution℠, you lay out your military campaign to overcome the common enemy so many businesses face: a failed succession plan.

A good example highlighting the importance of the *Mission Stage* can be seen in the experience of one of my favorite clients and friend. As an engineer, this business owner spent forty years developing his manufacturing facility to accommodate a single customer. For four decades, this single customer appreciated the services provided by my client. Business was profitable, and because he was able to devote all his energy to purchasing equipment and materials for one primary customer, my friend was successful.

The relationship took a critical turn, however, when the customer discovered my client did not have a succession plan. After forty years, the customer was now concerned about the future. If something happened to the engineer, what might happen to the continuous supply of product and great service his company had delivered over the years?

In this situation, my client was forced by his customer to address his succession plan. After our initial succession planning meeting, I recognized that identifying the client's *core principles* would be simple. My client did not have any family who would take over the business, so his succession goal was to make sure his employees continued to have gainful employment, and his aim was to find a new leader who would treat his workers with dignity and respect. His why for completing a succession plan was also simple: if he did not show his top customer a viable plan, he would likely lose his business. To me, this was a powerful *why*. The loss of his largest customer was his biggest risk, so his vision for a succession plan was to ensure the business would continue to run without his singular direction and daily involvement.

After developing the *why* and *what* of his plan, my client needed to develop the *how*—the central work of the *Mission Stage*. The business owner knew he had a great workforce and good managers, so he did not need to replace them. His accounting and financial systems were also operating efficiently. What the business lacked, however, was someone who could help generate additional customers and produce a new level of confidence with his principal customer. The business owner realized that he was acting as the company's CEO, COO, and CFO, and if his business was to survive, the succession plan had to start by reducing the business owner's central role in the company and broadening its client base.

After some deliberation, it was decided that the natural position to fill initially would be the role of COO. If the client could engage an effective COO, he would instill confidence in both his largest customer and in his employees. In addition, if the COO performed well, there would be a growth path to CEO. The next question was how to fill the role.

My client was a brilliant engineer and operations expert, but he had limited human resource skills. Thus, he engaged a consultant to help him define the skills a COO would need to possess, both from a qualitative and technical perspective. Once the job description was developed, the consultant continued to assist my client through the process of searching for a COO. After reviewing and interviewing a number of applicants, my client identified an outstanding candidate with both the operational and sales experience needed for the job.

First Step in the Mission Stage: Goal Setting

Establishing goals is central to the *Mission Stage*, and I am a firm believer in the SMART approach when it comes to setting goals. SMART is an acronym for Specific, Measurable, Agreed, Realistic, and Timely. The SMART approach can be used to set any goal, whether personal or business related.

We begin the process by selecting a *specific* goal. Without specificity, it's impossible to know with any certainty if a goal has been achieved. For instance, I may have a goal to lose weight to become healthier, but unless I have a specific number in mind, how will I know how much weight I want to lose? A goal must be *measurable* if you are to know when you have achieved it.

In business, you need facts and objectivity to determine if you are achieving your goals. I have found that almost all goals can be formulated so they allow for measurement. In fact, a goal that can't be measured can't be managed. For example, instead of having a goal to ensure your financial security, a more specific goal would be to establish a net worth you will require in order to retire securely. This is a manageable objective.

Similarly, your succession planning goals must be *agreed upon* if they are to be manageable. Even if you have a specific goal, if you don't have support from your team members, then stop and consider if it is the right goal. You may not need complete agreement, but if you are struggling unduly for consensus, then you need to question the goal's appropriateness. If, despite disagreement from your team members, you are confident you have the right goal, then I recommend you have a deeper conversation with those who disagree. As discussed in earlier chapters, implementing your goals becomes much harder when your team members do not agree with them. If someone on your team does not believe in the plan's goal, he or she will lack the passion or desire to achieve its objectives, which leads to an unnecessary drag on the entire succession process.

Next, your goals need to be *realistic*. I may have a goal to become the next quarterback for the Pittsburgh Steelers, and I may practice every day of the remainder of my life, but most people who know me would say I am not being realistic. Make sure your goals are within reach. Lastly, your goals must be *time-bound*. Without a date attached to them, your goals are nothing more than dreams. The *Mission Stage* is where you will set a time frame in which to achieve your goals.

Using the SMART approach to establish goals is your first step in the *Mission Stage*. You will want to develop specific, measurable, agreed upon, realistic, and timely goals for your succession plan. I recommend you begin by setting a time frame. Though the mission phase can cover any period you want, a three-year time horizon is ideal. Of course, there is no one-size-fits-all in succession planning, and only you can decide if a period longer than three years is appropriate for your specific situation.

I personally have found a three-year time frame to work better than a five-year structure, but this may not be the case for you. I prefer the shorter period because I want to clearly establish the actions I will take to achieve my goals within the time frame set. Moreover, I find when a time frame exceeds three years, the action steps often need to be adjusted in response to the ever-changing marketplace. In developing goals for the mission phase, refer back both to your ultimate goals for undertaking a succession plan and to any obstacles that surfaced during the challenge phase. These obstacles are the roadblocks to achieving your ultimate goals, so once you overcome them, achieving your long-term succession plan becomes easier.

As part of defining goals in the *Mission Stage*, you must ensure you possess and can dedicate the resources necessary to achieving your plan. General Schwarzkopf would not execute his mission unless and until he had the resources to complete the task. Similarly, you don't want to set a goal of hiring a CEO, CFO, and COO if your company does not have the resources to afford all three positions. A goal without a reasonable plan is nothing more than a fantasy that will only serve to frustrate both you and your team.

It is also common to develop too many goals in the mission phase of the succession planning process. Having too many goals is almost like having none. A recent meeting I held with a newly hired corporate associate illustrates this claim. When we hired this attorney, he had all the right skills and the right personality to deal with the closely-held clients our law firm represents. What's more, early in his employment, I was impressed that every time I asked if he could help me with a project, he eagerly accepted. At first, both our clients and I were impressed with his work and his ability to take on challenging tasks. After a few months, however, I began to notice the young lawyer was missing deadlines and making mistakes. When I inquired if everything was okay, he assured me he had everything under control. Unfortunately, things only got worse, and others began to see similar problems in the timing and quality of his work.

It is never an enjoyable task to speak with a colleague about his or her job performance, but I felt I owed it to this junior attorney to have a serious conversation. I wanted to know why he was becoming delinquent in submitting work when he had started out so well. I explained that others were losing confidence in him. I soon discovered what I had suspected: this eager young attorney had taken on too much work. Every time someone asked for help, he would accept the project—no matter its scope or the timeline involved. "I really like being needed," he shared. I explained that by saying yes to so many projects, he was actually saying no, because he could not keep up the pace. Thus, rather than pleasing clients, he was upsetting them. I explained as clearly as I could that as an attorney, time is his sole resource, and if he did not learn to use this resource judiciously, he was going to fail in his vocation.

Like this young lawyer, you can't focus on pleasing everyone on your team. You must be realistic in setting specific and timely goals as you complete the Mission Stage. Write down all goals you think you can complete in the specific time frame you have set. Don't worry about listing too many goals initially. Rather, list as many as you and your team think are appropriate. As with earlier stages, be sure these goals are documented and saved so they can be revisited as necessary. Once your goals are listed, prioritize the list, and shelve any goals that do not make the top five or six for another time. You may want to refer to them later, or they might make the next list once you've accomplished your first-tier goals. Right now is the time for triage.

There is no perfect or magic number of goals to list in the *Mission Stage*, but I would limit the list to your top five. Remember, in Operation Desert Storm, General Schwarzkopf had only a few goals. I am sure there were thousands of steps and tasks needed to complete the mission, but the General had a limited number of specific goals—to deploy the needed resources, to destroy the Iraqi air power and ability to communicate, and to attack.

Your goals should be similarly targeted. Carefully review your list and prioritize the most important goals you need to accomplish over the next three to five years; then select those goals that will take you closer to achieving the vision you established earlier in the process.

Second Step in the Mission Stage: Identifying and Confronting Obstacles

After you have listed and prioritized goals, the next step will be to identify the obstacles you will face in achieving your listed goals. You must always anticipate setbacks, detours, and impediments throughout the succession planning process. By anticipating obstacles, you will be better prepared to take on a challenge when it occurs. And, trust me, it will occur.

Obstacles also provide you with a choice. You can allow them to stop you or you can decide to take them on and overcome them. In this section of the form, the obstacles show you the way to your solution. As you did with your goals, try to list three to five obstacles you think you will face along the way.

Even though you may experience different obstacles or setbacks, any obstacle tends to provoke the same initial response: negativity. Many times, your response consists of fear, frustration, confusion, helplessness, depression or anger.

I have seen and experienced each one of these responses from business owners I have worked with. Heck, I have experienced and felt each one of these responses myself. You don't want to hide or deny these reactions. Rather, to achieve your succession plan, you need to identify them and understand they are natural and part of the process.

As mentioned in Chapter Two, it is estimated that 60 percent of all family business failures are due to lack of family communication and trust. Many families refuse to recognize and address fears and concerns when they experience a succession planning obstacle, which ultimately leads to failure.

The question is not whether concerns exist, but how will you deal with them once you identify them? Will you allow your concerns and fears to stop you, or will you choose a path to overcome them?

I believe the obstacles you identify become a map or GPS system to achieving your goals. You need to adopt the process of identifying them, determine what action you need to overcome them, and then have the determination to take them on.

For example, you may have decided on the ideal CEO for your business, but your wife wants someone else. She believes that your son or daughter should be the next CEO, even though neither of them is prepared. This can be a real obstacle for you. Once you have identified this obstacle, you now need to decide whether you want to address it or not. On the one hand, you must think about what is best for your business, but on the other hand, you do not want to upset your wife.

By ignoring the issue, you only prolong or delay the process. For many, the decision to ignore an issue is often preferable to confronting it. In this situation, I would suggest that if you simply recognize that it is natural to feel conflicted, you have made progress. The next step will take courage. Will you decide to face and address the obstacle, or will you decide to ignore it for the sake of family harmony? These are very difficult, but important, issues.

When identifying the obstacle on the form, don't try to figure out how to avoid or overcome the obstacle. Rather, at this stage, you simply want to identify major obstacles you and your stakeholders see in achieving your goals.

Once you and your team have listed all obstacles, decide whether or not you wish to take any or all of them on. The obstacles you decide to tackle should be listed on the form. It will be these obstacles that will help you decide on what actions you will need to take to achieve your goals. Your actions become the solution to your obstacle.

Third Step in the Mission Stage: Choosing Your Actions

Once you have identified and prioritized your *Mission Stage* goals and obstacles, you will then identify the specific actions that must be completed to get closer to achieving those goals and objectives. An unexecuted goal is worthless. In nearly every strategic planning process you will read about or experience, execution is the fundamental element for completing the strategic plan. A number of years ago, the *Harvard Business Review (HBR)* published the results of a study called the "Evergreen Project."[36] The study examined 160 successful companies to determine if common elements existed among them.

As you might imagine, many common elements were discovered. However, the study focused on three fundamental elements: (i) strategic planning, (ii) execution, and (iii) structure. For me, the primary value of this study is its reinforcement that even the greatest goals will not be achieved without developing *specific* steps for their attainment. Your succession plan is no different. To achieve its goals, you must develop specific actions, and then ensure that those steps are carried out.

Just as it is unwise to imagine you can act on your succession plan *without* specific goals, it is useless to have goals without a specific action plan. To use an analogy, you can spend days, weeks, or months in a jungle hacking down heavy bushes and underbrush in order to blaze your trail—but without a specific direction, you run the risk of going in circles, exhausting you and your team. Smart succession planners start with their goals, and then develop specific actions to achieve them. Actions follow goals; not the other way around.

Once you set your goals and determine your actions, you will have an executable action plan. When the plan has a defined purpose and a clear goal in mind, you and your team members will better understand the task before you, and your motivation will surge. Keep in mind that there is tremendous value in your succession plan, even if you discover some or all of your actions are not bringing you closer to your goals. Until you start to take action, you will never know which actions will work or will not work.

If you discover some of your actions are stalling, consider examining the issue at the next quarterly succession planning meeting. I once heard a YouTube executive speak wisely about mistakes. He said, "At YouTube, we treat mistakes as data to be used in updating our strategic planning process." Mistakes are data, and they can be used productively. In fact, The Succession Solution℠ process is designed for ongoing quarterly review, so until you and your team feel the plan has been achieved or is on the right trajectory, reviews are critical. Your *Mission Stage* steps can (and should) be updated, edited, and revised.

As previously stated, the actions you take to complete the *Mission Stage* of The Succession Solution[SM] should be designed to fulfill your established goals. However, during this phase, address the risks that were uncovered in the *Challenge Stage*. In other words, your mission phase goals should also be designed to mitigate the risks identified in earlier stages. It's essential to determine if the actions you've developed in this phase address earlier itemized risks.

For example, one of the common obstacles identified in the *Challenge Stage* by many business owners I have worked with over the years is a lack of competent next-generation leaders to take over the CEO's role. To address this risk, and to achieve the goal of identifying and developing the next generation of CEOs, a specific action plan may be required. One action plan may be to select one potential next-generation leader to obtain an MBA; another may be to have them develop an industry certification; and still another may be to have the potential leader participate in an in-house rotation system to learn each phase of your business.

There are a number of valuable consequences of establishing a specific plan to ensure you have a competent next-generation CEO. First, before anyone can take over as CEO, he or she will need the proper training to succeed. It would be unfair to the person and your organization to throw someone into such a role without suitable training. Second, an action plan that involves training shows the next generation you are willing to invest time and resources in that person. You are demonstrating that you have enough confidence in this next-generation leader to invest valuable resources for his or her success. Third, this action plan shows the rest of your organization (and possibly the outside world) that yours is the kind of forward-thinking company they want to work with.

Remember, too, there is value in this training process, even if the person turns out to be a complete failure, or it is determined that he or she is not right for the role. You may think a person is qualified, but you will never really know until you undertake the action of development. Further, if the person you select turns out to be unqualified, he or she will know they have been given a fair chance. In this case, an honest candidate will likely understand the situation and support the person who eventually succeeds to the new CEO role.

Another common goal for succession is to ensure your own financial security when you retire. For many of the folks I have worked with, this can be one of the most critical goals for a business owner. I believe that concern over financial wellbeing is one of the main reasons the existing generation of managers refuse to transition their role to the next generation—they are uncertain they will have enough money to retire!

Today, there are robust tools available to help provide you with clarity in determining your financial security. A good financial adviser can consider and analyze a variety of information to determine your "magic number" or the net assets needed to meet your goals.

While a younger generation may think their parents are "control freaks," sometimes the situation has nothing to do with control. Rather, it has to do with a senior generation's fear and uncertainty about finances. I recently met with a fifty-five-year-old business owner who had just sold his business. He told me that even though he has enough money to maintain his standard of living, he still gets nervous knowing he has no income coming from his business. He must live on the sale proceeds, a situation that still feels precarious to him. This business owner's candid admission helped me to see that understanding the psychology of the current generation of business owners is imperative for succession planning professionals. As a business owner, you need the confidence of knowing that you have enough money invested to enjoy your current lifestyle for the remainder of your life before you are willing to walk away from your current income.

Based on the goal of ensuring the financial security of the current generation, one action plan might be to develop a specific retirement package, one your company can afford. On the other hand, a stock redemption plan could be developed wherein you begin to liquidate or sell your stock. It is possible that you will be unable to ensure your financial security through a retirement plan or stock redemption, or there may be no real heir apparent for you. It is during the *Mission Stage* that you will want to address this issue. If your company cannot ensure your financial security, or if no competent successor exists, one goal at this stage may be to sell your company.

Selling your business can be a very effective succession plan strategy. Your succession plan is not a failure if you conclude that a sale of your business is better than a transfer to the next generation of owners. Rather, a sale may be the only way to ensure your business continues. If selling your business is part of the *Mission Stage* goals, and the best way to mitigate the risks of succession, you still want to establish an action plan for the transition of your business.

One client I worked with for years had no heir apparent and no one in his organization to take over his role as CEO. This client felt a close bond to his employees, acknowledging that without their hard work he could not have achieved his success. Thus, his succession planning goal was to locate a capable CEO from his industry to take over the business. Unfortunately, after three years of searching and interviewing candidates, he could not locate a candidate he felt comfortable with taking charge of the business and ensuring its success.

After his inability to locate a successor, the client engaged an investment banker to determine if he could locate a buyer to run the business successfully. At this stage of the business owner's life, he had already achieved financial independence. His main concern was the protection of his employees, which required the continued success of the business. Finally, after two years, the investment banker was able to find an individual who was interested in both buying the business and retaining the current employees. The client was very happy and felt he had achieved his succession planning goal of maintaining the business, which kept his name and protected his existing employees.

Most investment bankers or business brokers engaged in the sale of your business will advise you to begin preparing for the sale two to three years in advance. Selling your business can be a very effective succession plan if you have no one to leave your business to, or if you need the proceeds from the sale of your business to ensure your financial security in retirement.

As you work through the mission phase, remember that, just as you want to limit your goals, you also want to limit the actions taken to achieve your goals. Don't try to do too much! Don't try to "boil down the ocean," as some planners put it. Rather, as I suggested earlier, limit your mission actions to no more than five (or less, if possible).

Limiting your mission goals to three to five specific action steps each will give you the confidence you'll need to know you can accomplish more. Your success will also reduce the impulse to give up when frustrations arise.

Fourth Step in the Mission Stage: Measurements of Success

The final step in the *Mission Stage* of The Succession Solution[SM] is to develop what are often called Key Performance Indicators (KPIs). A Key Performance Indicator is an objectively-measured result that demonstrates how effective your company has been in achieving its key business objectives. Business owners typically use KPIs to evaluate their success in reaching targets and objectives.

In the *Mission Stage*, you will want to create your own succession KPIs based on the goals and actions you have established. Your KPIs will be indications of success, and no matter what goals you set, identify specific criteria to let you and your team know that you have attained the goal.

It is much better to establish KPIs early in the mission phase, because the stakeholders involved in your succession plan will normally decide as a group what results to achieve. Trying to determine the correct KPIs after action has already been taken can often lead to disagreement, discord, and anger. When your group tries to look for indicators of success without having thoughtfully considered beforehand what success should be, personal biases can creep in. As the old saying goes, figures don't lie, but liars figure. If you give shareholders a chance to justify a situation in retrospect, they may be prone to rationalize their decision, despite its limited value. However, if your group determines ahead of time what KPI (or yardstick) to use to measure success, then there will be less acrimony over its use. There will always be less confusion and argument when you establish KPIs ahead of time.

For example, one of your succession plan goals could be to assign more client responsibility to a certain person or member of the founder's family. The action may be to introduce this person to a specific number of clients to gain their confidence, and for them to assume full client responsibility. Based on these stated goals and actions, a KPI may be to officially record the number of clients for whom this person is now fully accountable for sales and service. This number should not be hard to track and will be a good indicator of whether or not this person is achieving the goal established by the team.

While the established KPI may be an indicator of success, it should not be viewed as determinative. KPIs are established to track and evaluate results. If the results don't match the level initially hoped for, there may be valid reasons for why. Lack of immediate success may indicate that some form of additional action is required. For instance, it may be that more training is needed, or the selected employee may have been assigned the most difficult client to handle, or some other fact may surface that is important to evaluating the assessment process. Nevertheless, KPIs must be designed for the *Mission Stage* so that measurement criteria are in place for quarterly reviews of the succession plan.

When I was young, my friends and I would often play football in someone's backyard. As you might imagine, none of my friends' backyards had defined boundaries or end zone markers. Rather, we would use a tree, fence, or simply throw down some piece of clothing to make the end zone or indicate out-of-bounds. We had to establish these lines of demarcation before we started. Otherwise, the game would end in a huge fight, which it still did at times—arguing over exactly where a particular tree was planted. Regardless, we all knew we had to set some standards for success before the game started to avoid most of the disputes that would occur later.

For similar reasons, you need to develop your measurements of success before you begin your succession plan so you can avoid an argument after the fact about someone stepping out of bounds when they completed their task.

Mission (3 Years)

10. Goals

- Next CEO in place
- Prior CEO transfer to Chairman of the Board
- Board created with various family members

11. Obstacles

- Existing CEO needs retirement package
- Existing Board resistant to change
- Family shareholders don't agree on next CEO

12. Actions

- Create retirement package for existing CEO
- Shareholders consensus as to new Board
- Board hires next CEO

13. Measurements of Success (KPIs)

- Board meetings working on succession plan
- New CEO in place
- Retirement plan completed
- New independent BOD member added

Keys to Chapter

1. The Mission Stage is where you will establish your three-to-five-year goals to accomplish, which will address your obstacles and opportunities and move you closer to your long-term vision.

2. Use the SMART (Specific, Measurable, Agreed, Realistic, and Timely) approach when developing your goals to ensure you know when you have achieved them.

3. Develop actions steps you will take to move closer to your goals.

4. Use KPIs (Key Performance Indicators) to track the performance or lack of performance your actions are making on your succession plan.

CHAPTER FOURTEEN: THE ANNUAL REVIEW STAGE

"He who chases two hares catches neither"

– Erasmus's Adages

In the *Annual Review Stage*, you will develop the goals, actions, and KPIs you generated during the *Mission Stage* into a more specific action plan that will unfold over the next twelve months. This plan moves you ever closer to your long-term goals, which will ultimately lead to the successful completion of your succession plan.

As a successful business owner, you have likely developed some system, formal or otherwise, to deal with daily, weekly, or monthly emergencies that arise. You would not have the successful business you do today if you didn't have processes in place for dealing with urgent matters. However, you cannot afford to focus on immediate and/or urgent goals alone. For example, a client contract that requires the delivery of a certain product at a certain time in order to avoid delay of a major job is both important and urgent. A text message from a buddy who wants you to join him for golf later that day may be urgent but it is likely not important (unless, of course, it's an invitation to play the Augusta National—at which point the invitation is both urgent and important!).

It is true that succession planning will not ring your phone or send you a text message demanding that you deal with a particular problem, but this just reinforces my point. This is why using The Succession Solution℠ is so valuable—it provides the necessary tools and reminders you will need to follow the succession planning process through to a successful conclusion. The *Annual Review Stage* invites you to both set and monitor the goals, actions, and KPIs you will need to meet every year until your succession plan has been positively achieved.

Some strategic planning experts claim that intrinsic conflicts exist between long-term planning and short-term tactics. When management teams focus on accomplishing short-term objectives, these authorities contend, they forget about their long-term goals. The Succession Solution^{SM} is designed to tackle these tensions by helping you advance successfully between long-and short-terms goals. The annual review phase in particular is a powerful tool that allows you to establish and reconcile both the long-and short-term goals necessary to achieve your overall goals for succession.

As you progress through this stage of The Succession Solution^{SM}, your long-term goals work in concert with your short-term tactics, because these more immediate strategies are designed to support your greater objectives. Short-term aims, then, must always be set within the larger context of long-term intentions. You know that short-term goals cannot be well developed without first defining the bigger picture. Moreover, a lack of long-term goals can cause you to become slaves to the daily distractions and emergencies that unfailingly occur. One absolute fact I have learned over thirty years as an entrepreneur, certified public accountant, and attorney is that as soon as you remedy one emergency or crisis, another will eventually appear! Don't let the emergencies of the moment overwhelm your long-term goals.

Annual Goals

The first step in the *Annual Review Stage* is to develop the particular succession planning goals you want to accomplish within the next year. Of course, as with all phases of The Succession Solution^{SM}, you must avoid the temptation to set too many goals at this stage, for when we try to accomplish too much, we often achieve nothing. I suggest you list no more than five goals to complete in a year.

Before you develop your annual goals, reexamine each of the goals developed during the *Mission Stage* and decide which of these objectives—or which component of a particular goal—you want to achieve within the next year. This reexamination may help you recognize that one target must be accomplished before another can be achieved. For instance, if one of your goals is to retire within the next three to five years, and another goal is to hire a chief operating officer (COO) to help with your transition, focusing on locating a COO would precede your retirement.

By reviewing the goals developed in the *Mission Stage*, you can generate short-term (twelve month) aims designed to move you ever closer to attaining longer-term goals that will culminate in the successful achievement of your succession plan. As you develop these twelve-month goals, you may discover that you've listed too many goals. You may even feel overwhelmed by the total number of short-range goals that must be accomplished to move closer to your longer-term goals. Don't be discouraged, however, because this long list is tangible evidence that you are on the right track.

Once your list of twelve-month goals has been generated, it is time to do a little triage. Examine the entire record and decide on your top three to five goals to complete over the next year. Keep in mind that successful achievement of your goals will require you to dedicate the necessary time and resources, so factor in these assets as well. Remember, too, that it is wiser to accomplish fewer goals than to take on so many that you're unable to achieve them all. You want to celebrate your successes rather than wallow in your setbacks!

Just as you did during earlier stages of the planning process, document and save all formulated goals that did not make the year-one cut. These objectives may become your next priorities once you've achieved your first concerns, or they may become your top annual goals for the following year. Keep in mind that in this context there are never unrealistic goals, only unrealistic timeframes.

Once your objectives have been listed and prioritized, I suggest you put the uppermost annual goal first and proceed accordingly. While each of your top three to five goals will be important, it is still necessary to prioritize. Ask yourself, "What would have to happen for me to sit here twelve months from today and feel good about my progress?" Remember that even if your top three to five goals take more than twelve months to complete, the mere fact that you have identified and listed them is very powerful. I have found that most business owners complete their annual goals sooner than predicted, for once a task is listed and identified, most business owners will work to complete it. I believe this is because their entrepreneurial skills and drive for success naturally kick in to get the task done!

When developing your annual goals, each of the three to five goals listed should meet the SMART criteria (Specific, Measurable, Agreed upon, Realistic, and Time-targeted). By following the SMART principles, you'll have a much better chance of determining both how you will achieve your goals and if you have attained them. Remember that unless you have some objective criteria to determine the accomplishment of a particular goal, you will likely become distracted by another seemingly more urgent matter. Moreover, without benchmarks for evaluating a goal's success, you may convince yourself you have completed a goal that you have not. This work is not easy, and we often look for ways to turn our attention to simpler tasks.

Another benefit of creating SMART goals is the service they provide in formally completing the *Annual Review Stage* of The Succession Solution[SM] and delegating tasks. Of course, I am not suggesting you create SMART goals merely to finalize the process; rather, I am saying that the proper completion of each phase of The Succession Solution[SM] will dramatically increase your chance of enjoying a powerful succession plan.

An even more important reason to develop SMART goals is that they help you delegate the duties necessary to complete them. In the *Annual Review Stage*, as in the *Quarterly Review Stage*, you begin to assign tasks to the individuals best suited to each particular job. To avoid confusion and potential conflict as to whether a goal has been achieved, the "SMARTer" the goal, the better it will be for you and your team. If your annual goals are well defined and agreed upon in advance, their accomplishment should not be subject to much debate. Everyone on your team ought to know whether or not that goal has been met. The more a goal is left to interpretation, however, the more likely you will encounter confusion and debate. As the saying goes, beauty is in the eye of the beholder. If we set a goal that is subjective and not easily quantified, we may discover that others genuinely believe they have accomplished a goal when it is clear to you that they have not. Thus, using precise language and carefully aligning the right goal with the right team member is crucial at this stage.

Sharing Your Annual Goals

After developing your annual goals, consider sharing then with both family and team members who were not part of the planning process. It is often helpful to gain the insight and feedback of these individuals. While your succession plan must begin with you, including as much of the team as possible as you work to accomplish these vital tasks over the next twelve months can be very beneficial.

When you review your annual goals with family and team members and seek their feedback, you also want to let them know that you're taking a very important step in achieving a sturdy succession plan for the company. This disclosure gives you, your family, and your team the confidence and insight needed to confront the future.

Helping your family and team members understand their current and potential future roles in your company will motivate them to participate in the succession planning process.

Alternatively, when your family or team members do not like what they see and can't accept or change it, then it might be time to address the issue. Owners in a family business often avoid conflict until it is too late, but unaddressed problems rarely go away on their own. Instead, they fester and get bigger and harder to deal with. We see this in our geo-political world, as well as in our personal lives, so why would it be different in our businesses?

Frequently, business owners dodge conflict because they realize they may have to deal with a particular person at a family event, or that person has an important relationship with another family member. For instance, you or your spouse may not want to deal with the conflict of deciding on a successor among your children and/or in-laws. Real concerns may arise if you select one child over another, and you may lose a personal relationship with your family members or grandchildren. Legitimate struggles occur when you know the correct business decision but avoid making it because you fear your choice will impact a personal relationship.

A problem for the current generation will become a problem for the next. It is staggering how many family members in their forties and fifties do not know what succession plan is in place for the family business—or if there is a plan at all! The next leader's uncertainty about their role in the future of the company is both stressful and unfair, for it can lead to debilitating circumstances for them.

I have often found the longer you wait to decide on difficult succession planning issues, the fewer options exist for you. This phenomenon occurs because even as you try to decide what to do or how to do it, others make decisions on their own. They get frustrated waiting for you to decide. Eventually, they refuse to wait for you to decide and leave to pursue other opportunities.

I was asked a number of years ago to help the founder of a very large family-owned food distribution company. The founder started the business back when he had practically nothing. He ultimately created one of the biggest food distribution companies in the area. He had two sons working in the business who were extremely competent and were running the business without much direction from the founder. After years of talking about succession planning, the founder refused to take any action. Exasperated, irritated, and annoyed by the founder's lack of action, one of the two brothers left the business to start a competing business. The founder not only lost one of his two potential successors, but the business declined in revenue. The son's departure to start a competing business tore the family apart. The founder, however, still refused to take any succession planning action. Unfortunately, the remaining son became ill and was unable to take over the business. A few years later, the business was no longer in the family. This is an unfortunate example of how options diminish the longer you wait to plan for succession.

In the past, I have always asked each of the employers I have worked with to tell me when I am not right for a particular job. I have candidly requested that they tell me if I am screwing up. I do this because I can use this information to make an informed decision about what to do next. The same approach can be used in your business. Once you tell a family member that he or she will *not* be the next one in charge, they can decide from an informed position to leave or stay. I believe it is always fairer to let your employees and family members know the situation, so they can make decisions about the future in their own best interest.

I think it is selfish not to let the next generation of family members or employees know what your plans are for the future. How would you feel if you were working on your career only to discover that you are laboring under a false sense of expectations? I have found that keeping your team and family members in the dark can be a recipe for disaster. Unquestionably, succession issues can produce very difficult discussions, but it is better to confront these challenges *before* they become more serious problems than to wait until you are no longer around to address them.

Obstacles

Once you have identified your top three to five goals you want to achieve during the next year, it is time to move on to identifying the obstacles that stand in the way of achieving your one-year goals. As you did in the *Mission Stage*, you want to list the obstacles that are preventing you from achieving your one-year goals. Don't list an obstacle you are not willing to tackle. You need to have courage to accept many of the obstacles, because overcoming them all is not to be guaranteed.

I promise that if you do decide to take on an obstacle and succeed in overcoming it, then your team and your company will be that much stronger. Your entire group will be stronger because you have overcome the obstacle holding you back from your goals and because you proved that you had the courage to accept the challenge in order to improve the company. They will be better because they learned from the process.

The first business I created was a legal staffing company called Legal Network. While we were ultimately very successful, we certainly did not start well. When we began, we were very conservative with our finances. We took this approach because we were uncertain if our new business would work.

After losing money in our first year of operations, we began to question whether the business model would work. By accident, we met another owner of a legal staffing company located in Denver, Colorado, who offered to provide us guidance. When we met with him, he told us we had a terrible location, no leadership, and less-than-stellar employees. What a kick in the gut that was. I think his comments hurt so badly because they were all true.

After that meeting, we decided our greatest and most critical obstacle to success was finding a strong CEO. We knew if we did not commit the necessary resources to hire a CEO, the business had no chance of survival. As a result, we developed a job description for a CEO and committed the resources needed to hire a qualified candidate. Within three months, we had hired our first CEO. Once we brought the CEO on board, we experienced growth and profitability every year.

This is an example of identifying an obstacle and having the courage to confront it. While we were uncertain if hiring a CEO would work, we knew the company would fail if we did not act.

During this section of the process, discuss and identify all obstacles that could hold you back from reaching your annual goals. I would not recommend you try to list every obstacle possible, however. Rather, try to list only the top three to five obstacles you are willing to work on during the year.

Actions

After developing your goals for the upcoming year and identifying the obstacles preventing you from reaching those goals, the next step in the *Annual Review Stage* is to decide on the actions that must be taken to meet those objectives. Each annual goal that is set during this stage will have a clear action attached to it. You and your team must determine what specific action is needed to accomplish each goal. The "goals" section of the *Annual Review Stage* is where you will list at least one action for each recorded goal. Identifying a specific action item that will get you closer to each goal will drive forward your overall succession planning process.

Keep in mind that goals without actions are nothing but dreams. As an astute business owner, you know that there is little room for unattainable dreams in the business world. Your business is too important not to have an action plan.

Clear actions become the tactics you undertake to accomplish your annual goals. The term "tactic" is defined as an *action carefully planned to achieve a specific end.* Thus, if a strategy represents the long-term action you will take to accomplish a goal, your tactics are the short-term steps you must take to move closer to your longer-term goals. Ask yourself, "What specific steps must I take to achieve my established annual goals?" Your answer will indicate the appropriate actions to focus upon during the upcoming year to make sure you are supporting your plan by allocating the resources necessary to achieving your goals.

A few years ago, I was an owner of a national residential real estate closing company that had the responsibility of scheduling and coordinating real estate closings all over the United States. We had the responsibility of scheduling thousands of loans each month in conjunction with a network of attorneys whom we would schedule to attend each closing to ensure the mortgage was properly finalized and that loan documents were correctly recorded.

Most people who refinance their mortgages want to schedule their closings during the last few days of the month. This is because when buyers finalize a loan on a particular day of the month, at the closing, the bank (or mortgage company) will require that daily interest for that loan be paid through the end of the month. Since the bank will not receive its mortgage payment until the following month, loan officials oblige buyers to prepay the per diem interest on the loan. Thus, when buyers close earlier in the month, they pay more interest than they would near month's end.

To avoid paying any more interest than necessary, most borrowers wanted to close at the end of the month. As a result of circumstances beyond our control, then, as our business grew, it became increasingly difficult to accommodate every customer who wanted to close in the last week of the month. Moreover, if we could not schedule a closing that fit our borrowers' conditions, they would seek an alternative closing company. At one point, we were losing nearly 25 to 30 percent of our business because we had become too busy. Can you imagine how frustrated we felt? Like most owners, we wanted additional business, but in our situation, we couldn't schedule all the work offered to us.

During a strategy planning meeting, we identified this loss of business as both a threat and an opportunity—true of so many obstacles that exist in business. We realized that if we did not provide our customers with their required closing date, they would seek alternatives, and another competitor might step in. We decided that our goal for the next twelve months would be to increase our closing ratio from 75 to 80 percent.

After setting this closing goal, we decided to share it with everyone in the organization. We believed that if everyone was aware of our intention and made it "top of mind," we could increase our closing ratio. Accordingly, one of our tactics became to place on the home page of every computer in the company both the overall 80 percent closing-rate target and the actual closing ratio for each month. We also provided bonuses for our employees when we achieved our closing goal.

Everyone in the company began focusing on this goal. When an order came in from a customer, an employee would schedule the closing as soon as possible. As a result of this concentrated mission, we achieved our objective within a year. This is an example of an action that can be taken to support a goal.

Sometimes the smallest actions can start a process that results in tremendous results. Never discount what is known as the "butterfly effect," for I have witnessed it happen many times in the succession planning process. The butterfly effect is an often-used example that illustrates how an apparently small initial difference can lead to large unforeseen consequences over time. In fact, some meteorologists contend that great winds and storms can be initiated by a single flap of a butterfly's wings!

Let me share an example that illustrates the key role small actions can have in the larger goal of succession planning. Not long ago, a second-generation minority shareholder came to me frustrated by his father's refusal to cede control. The son was extremely competent and had been operating the company for years. He knew the company's organizational documents were not in good order and would create problems when his father, the majority shareholder, passed away. He also knew that his father had gifted stock to other family members who were not involved in the business. As a result, in the event of his passing, the working son could end up laboring for these uninvolved siblings.

With this concern in mind, the son engaged me to assist the company in a succession planning process. While the father was initially resistant to the idea of succession planning, he agreed to participate. Both the son and I knew that if we set bold goals for succession, the father may abandon the entire process, so we developed a slow but clearly-defined process.

One of our goals during the first year was merely to review and update the company's organizational documents, including the company's articles of incorporation, by-laws, shareholder agreements, and stock certificates. During this review, it was revealed to the father how his son, who had spent twenty years in the business, could lose control of the company to his siblings at the father's passing.

Because the facts of our findings were delivered by me and not the son, the father did not view the information as being biased or slanted to benefit his son. Moreover, since the father was a smart business owner, he realized something had to be done. Eventually, the business-involved son structured a buy-out of his parents' business and avoided potential sibling rivalry.

This is an example of how one small action item can have a butterfly effect. By beginning the *Annual Review Stage* with the goal of updating the company's organizational documents, the company's succession plan was accomplished. Although reviewing structural documents may seem mundane or unimportant, I am always amazed by what a review of these materials can produce in terms of results for clients.

Measurements of Success

Once you have identified actions for each of your listed annual goals, the next step in the process is to list the measurements you'll use to determine success—measurements we called Key Performance Indicators (KPIs) in the prior chapter. I recently heard someone refer to KPIs as the "trophy numbers" of a business, because they are used to determine a company's success in achieving its annual goals. Although you and your team members need only a few good measurements of success, assessment tools utilize objective criteria that can both point to the right track and ensure that you're on it.

Let me share an example. I had a client who was a second-generation family member who was concerned with his father's role in the business. My client was the only one of three siblings working in the family business. He knew that his parents had not updated their will in decades, and that, in its current state, the will divided everything equally among the three children. As a result, our annual goal was to have his parents update their estate plan. The initial action item set to accomplish this goal was to have his parents meet with their attorney and accountant to review both their estate plan and its tax effects. One measurement of success for this goal was to have his parents' estate plan completed and current.

In this situation, the parents wanted to treat all of their children equally with respect to the value of their estate. While it was clear that they wanted the business-involved son to inherit the stock in the company, it was determined after meeting with their accountant that the business's net worth exceeded the son's share of his expected inheritance. As a result, until the parents had the opportunity to transfer the business to their son, their updated wills stipulated that if the son wanted to inherit all of the stock in the company, he would need to pay his siblings the difference between his one-third share and the value of the company stock.

In this succession planning process, the client's measurement of success was the completion of his parents' estate plan to give him insight into the future. Fortunately, in the following year, his parents began a plan to sell the business to this next generation business owner.

Caution: Reasons You Can Fail

As you continue to get more specific with your goals and actions, you need to be vigilant as to how your plan might go off track. Keeping your focus on your annual goals and actions is critical, and this will occur only if you meet every ninety days.

Your plans can also be upset when key stakeholders in your organization don't understand the action items you have selected, or why they have been selected. Thus, as emphasized earlier, it is crucial to share with significant team and family members both your succession planning goals and why you have selected your specific annual aims and tactics. Your chances of success are greatly increased when important team members are aware of the goals you have set. As you recall with the real estate closing company, we went as far as placing our goal on everyone's desktop home page. Some might argue that our action was a bit extreme, but it worked! Your stakeholders need to know where you are going and if you want them to follow confidently.

A second caution I offer is not to make your goals or actions too complicated. When developing your goals and tactics, use the KISS (Keep It Simple, Stupid) approach. When you keep your plan basic and begin the process with the support and confidence of your team, you will be amazed by how the butterfly effect can lead to unexpected and remarkable consequences in your succession plan.

My third caution is to remind you to budget for your plan. It is unlikely that you will achieve your stated goals if you don't allocate the mandatory resources in time or money. Succession goals are no different than any other goals you set in business. If you want your sales people to become more effective, you can't expect them to improve sales results without providing them the proper tools or training. Your succession plan goals are no different. Once you establish your annual goals and action items, determine the resources you must allocate to ensure success.

For example, if your goal is to determine the value of your business for the purposes of selling or gifting a portion of the business to the next generation, engage a business valuation specialist. Moreover, when obtaining a business valuation, budget money for the appraiser and know that the appraisal will take a few months to complete.

Lastly, I suggest that once your annual goals and actions are set, you go back and test them against your ultimate succession goals or visions. We can sometimes lose the forest for the trees.

Annual Review

15. Goals

- Management provides CEO recommendations
- Shareholders' consensus on new Board member
- Develop CEO role and compensation plan

16. Obstacles

- Inactive Board
- CEO uncertain about financial situation
- Shareholder discord

17. Actions

- Meet with management regarding CEO
- CEO meets with financial planner
- List key customer relationships with CEO

18. Measurements of Success (KPIs)

- Shareholders agree to new Board
- List of key customers provided with a transition plan to introduce prospective CEO

Keys to Chapter

1. From your list of three-year goals, decide which goals you want to accomplish in the next twelve months.

2. As with your three-year goals, use the SMART approach with your one-year goals to measure success, failure, or the need to readjust.

3. Don't try to boil the ocean. Rather, try to achieve three to five goals within a twelve-month period.

4. Prioritize your goals by importance. Decide on the goals you want to achieve within the next twelve months.

CHAPTER FIFTEEN: THE QUARTERLY REVIEW STAGE

"Long-term goals are achieved through the accomplishments of short-term tactics."

– Bradley J. Franc

"Vision without execution is hallucination." These words belong to the great inventor and businessman Thomas Edison. The *Quarterly Review Stage* of The Succession Solution℠ is designed to support the completion and execution of your succession plan. In chapter thirteen, I referred to an HBR study which reviewed the common elements linking 160 successful companies. As you may recall, these three shared elements were: (i) strategic planning, (ii) execution, and (iii) structure. Now is the time to create the specific actions, tasks, and steps you must accomplish in ninety-day increments until your plan has been fully realized. The *Quarterly Review Stage* is the ultimate execution stage of your succession plan. If you don't complete and execute at this stage, it will be very difficult to accomplish your goals.

By now, you have come very far in the planning process, and you should be proud of what you have accomplished. However, if you lose momentum at the quarterly review phase of the process, you run a great risk of not crossing the finish line. Too many organizations develop brilliant and strategic succession plans filled with bells and whistles, only to uncover those plans years later—covered in dust! Obviously, if you don't execute your plan it will remain unrealized.

I have encountered numerous abandoned plans over the years, and interestingly, the cause for their abandonment had little to do with their overall viability. Instead, these plans remained unfulfilled due to the business owners' inability to act and remain accountable. Nothing can be accomplished without some action, and the main reason succession plans fail is an inability on the part of owners and team members to execute and follow up on their plans' progress.

Paradoxically, executing your plan leads to success—regardless of the outcome—because every step you take keeps you moving forward. Obviously, when you identify and successfully complete a particular quarterly task, you move closer to fulfilling your succession plan. But even when you develop a quarterly task that does *not* move you closer to your goals, it is still a success if you learn from the mistake. The inherent value of setting and executing quarterly tasks is that it keeps you committed to the process, and as long as you maintain that resolve, you will achieve your succession goals.

Learning the Value of Quarterly Reviews

After graduating from the Pennsylvania State University, I began my professional career at the accounting firm of Arthur Young and Company in Pittsburgh. Back in the 1980s, this company was one of eight accounting firms (known as the "Big 8") that provided accounting, tax, and auditing services to the world's most prestigious corporations. In fact, many CEOs and presidents of today's Fortune 1,000 companies began their careers at one of these eight accounting firms. Today, as a result of mergers and consolidations, there are only four major accounting firms who audit over 80 percent of U.S. public companies. They are Deloitte, PricewaterhouseCoopers, EY, and KPMG.

For an accounting major, obtaining employment at a Big 8 company was the best job one could get right out of college. These firms provided their employees with the finest training and experience one could obtain in the field. I couldn't have found a better place to start my business career in accounting.

I was a junior in college when I began to hear and learn about the Big 8. Everyone told me that securing a job at such a firm would be my ticket to fame and fortune (heck, they even show up at the Oscars). Not knowing any better, I set my goals on landing a job at one of these firms. During the last two years of college, I worked to improve my grades, practiced mock interviews, and even spent my savings to invest in a nice business suit, tie, and shirt. That's all I could afford at the time, so I treated them like the valuable assets they were.

After interviewing with the eight firms, I was fortunate to receive an offer of employment from Arthur Young and Company, now known as EY. Although several of the better students received many more offers, since I could only work for one firm, I felt my goal had been achieved. Although I received tremendous training and education at Arthur Young and Company, over time I realized that I was not enjoying my work as much as I had expected. As a young CPA, it was not unusual to work seven days a week, ten hours a day—all of the Big 8 firms exacted their pound of flesh!

So, there I was, having spent the better part of my undergraduate years trying to secure a job with one of the Big 8 firms, only to discover that I did not like the work. To make matters worse, I was working more hours than I had ever imagined. I think the only thing that kept me going was the fact that I had no money after graduating from college, so I didn't have the luxury of quitting to "find myself."

I felt stuck and frustrated because I wasn't sure how I was going to change my situation. I'd never felt so lost. I am not sure how it happened or who might have suggested this to me, but I decided to take a few days off to consider my situation and plan for my future. I found a quiet cubicle in the University of Pittsburgh's Hillman Library where I wouldn't be distracted or disturbed, and I put together a very rough outline of what I wanted to do and how I was going to achieve my goal. It was my first serious goal-setting session, and it turned out to be one of the best investments of my time in my young professional career.

After that daylong meeting with myself, I was reinvigorated. I finally had a tentative plan for my future. Again, for reasons I am not certain I could explain, I decided to reschedule a similar meeting with myself in three months, and I continued to reschedule regular meetings until I was able to take my next concrete step.

Since those days of quiet self-reflection at the Hillman Library back in the early 1980s, I have continued to schedule quarterly meetings with myself in one form or another. You might think I am a little crazy, but I can state with complete confidence that these sessions have become an extraordinarily valuable use of my time for both business and personal purposes.

I will make one admission, however: there have been a number of quarters over the years in which I was unable to schedule a meeting. Still, I learned from these missed opportunities as well, for every time I missed a quarterly meeting, I could see my progress slowing down.

Why Meet Quarterly?

In his best-selling book, *The 12 Week Year*, Brian P. Moran states that we should all plan our personal, as well as business goals, around a twelve week period. Moran states, "The great thing about the twelve week year is that the deadline is always near enough that you never lose sight of it. It provides a time horizon that is long enough to get things done, yet short enough to create a sense of urgency." Similarly, The Succession Solution^{SM} uses quarters instead of twelve weeks to achieve and implement your succession plan.

Quarterly meetings can be powerful, life-changing exercises for you and your team. I recommend them to all of my clients and have used them in all the businesses I've started. In fact, as a condition of my accepting a succession planning engagement, the client must agree in advance to meet with me on a quarterly basis throughout the first year.

It is no surprise to you that the demands of daily business can distract you from your larger goals. We are all easily diverted by the unpredictable emergencies that demand our immediate attention. Thus, to achieve long-term and/or big goals and objectives, you must have a process in place, so you don't forget about these goals or trick yourself into thinking you will get to them "someday." Quarterly meetings ensure that you keep your most important matters on the radar.

I discovered that quarterly meetings provide just enough time to determine if real progress is being made on set goals. I also learned that quarterly meetings offer the right amount of time to recognize any errors, and they also allow time for readjustment.

Meeting more often than ninety days is too quick and doesn't afford the time necessary to see if progress is being made. It is like digging up the soil to see if the roots are growing. The ninety-day period is a long enough time to evaluate whether or not what you are doing is moving you closer to your goals or if you need to self-correct.

I have witnessed clients who decide to meet on an annual basis to discuss their succession plan, and the result is that day-to-day issues have overtaken the importance of their plan. Hard stuff is too easy to postpone. Few of us want to schedule that dentist appointment, colonoscopy, or annual physical. However, we set these appointments and complete the procedures because we know failing to have them done could prove deadly.

Another challenge that arises from waiting a year or so to review your plan is determining if family and team members agree on what action plans may or may not be working. Wouldn't you rather discover you are off course after ninety days rather than after a year or so?

Stephen Covey talks about the importance of constantly readjusting our goals and action plans by using an airplane analogy:

> The plane takes off at the appointed hour toward that predetermined destination. But in fact, the plane is off course at least 90 percent of the time. Weather conditions, turbulence, and other factors cause it to get off track. However, feedback is given to the pilot constantly, who then makes course corrections and keeps coming back to the exact flight plan, bringing the plane back on course. And often, the plane arrives at the destination on time. It's amazing. Think of it. Leaving on time, arriving on time, but off course 90 percent of the time. If you can, create this image of an airplane, a destination, and a flight plan in your mind…[37].

Meeting on a quarterly basis allows you to bring your succession plan back on track every few months. When you don't meet on a quarterly basis, you can't obtain the feedback all plans need to stay the course, and this can lead to frustration with your lack of success or worse—you may not even realize you've been focused on the wrong things. On the other hand, if you choose to meet too often—monthly, for instance—you can get frustrated with the lack of progress. This is why I termed the last step in The Succession Solution℠, the *Quarterly Review Stage.*

Let me also note that it is at this stage in the succession planning process that the real action and fun start for you and your team. This is when you begin to see tangible results happening, and it's incredibly motivating for you and your team to see the plan come into action. As Colonel John "Hannibal" Smith often said on the 1980s television show *The A-Team*, "I love it when a plan comes together."

Completing the Quarterly Review Stage

At this point, you and your team have developed your three-and one-year goals, actions, and measurements of success. Now it is time to decide on the three to five actions you will work on during the next quarter. To determine these, begin by reviewing your annual goals. What short-term steps can be taken to move you closer to accomplishing your annual goals? What is preventing you from achieving your annual goals? It's been said that "it isn't the mountains ahead to climb that wear you out, it's the pebble in your shoe."

As you begin this process, start with a few tasks only—three to five at most. As the Chinese fable teaches us, if you want to move mountains, you must begin by removing small stones. What small stones do you want to remove to move your mountain? You should be able to reasonably accomplish these three or so tasks within the next ninety days. And don't forget, you will have to allocate the appropriate resources to accomplish these tasks. As we've said earlier, when a task is important to you, you must be willing to earmark the appropriate resources. This dedication of resources can be in the form of people, money, or some other investment. Moreover, if you are unable to support a particular task with the appropriate level of resources, then postpone listing that task until you can secure the needed resources.

Try to be as specific as possible in listing each quarterly task. Remember that you will want to determine the success or failure of a particular task at the next meeting, so if you list a task that is hard to measure, beware of creating uncertainty among your team. Think about the SMART analogy discussed earlier, and be sure your quarterly tasks are specific, measurable, agreed upon, realistic, and timely. If you follow this standard, you will have an objective task that can be measured for progress.

After you have listed your quarterly tasks, identify a responsible party to take charge of each. A responsible party is not necessarily the person who must complete the task. Rather, the responsible party is the person who accepts the task, reports on it at the next quarterly meeting, and determines what assets must be in place to get the job done. It is the responsible party who determines if the task is achievable in the next quarter, so this person must be given the time, resources, and autonomy to complete the task. Furthermore, it will be the responsible party's duty to report if he or she does not have the interest to accomplish these goals, or the time, resources, and authority required to bring them to fruition.

Once the actions are identified and the responsible parties are named, you then want to list the success criteria. What must happen to determine if the quarterly priorities are being achieved? For instance, if one of your priorities is to develop a family employment policy, the success criteria may be that a draft of the policy is presented to you for review.

Celebrate Your Success

The next step in the *Quarterly Review Stage* is to decide on a way to celebrate success. If you achieve quarterly tasks, what celebration or reward do you and your team want? I have seen clients reward their team with lunch, dinner, golf, or tickets to a sporting event. It is not the actual event that really matters, but the value of taking time out to celebrate the achievement of certain goals. There is a lot of value in recognizing the contributions of others. By acknowledging team members publicly and celebrating your company's success, you will likely have a more motivated group at your next ninety-day meeting.

Even small celebrations of success are important, because they commemorate collective achievements. Recognizing your team's efforts brings the members closer together, and this promotes deeper understanding across the board. Part of a family (and any other closely-held) business is to have a little fun. Shared enjoyment can enhance the overall process of succession planning. What's more, this feeling of common purpose becomes especially important when times of disappointment arise and when arguments occur. If you have bonded a little during the celebration periods, you may find your team is able to pull together and overcome some of the more challenging times ahead. Stephen Covey would call this exercise making "emotional bank account deposits."

Scheduling the Next Quarterly Meeting

The last step in the succession planning process is to set the next meeting date. Successful people are also busy people, so if you wait sixty to ninety days to set the next meeting date, you may find some of the key people at your last meeting cannot make the next. One of the top mistakes business owners and family members make is not having the same team members at subsequent meetings. What can happen in this instance is the missing team member is blamed for any existing problems, and this can stall or derail the process.

Let's face it, everyone has a busy schedule, so commit to scheduling meeting dates in advance. Set the date for the next meeting at the end of each quarterly meeting. I assure you that the time spent will be well worth the effort. Scheduling the next meeting is not only efficient, it demonstrates shared commitment. Try not to end any quarterly meeting without being sure to schedule the next one.

I have to admit that it drives me crazy to hear people say they do not have time to meet or that they do not have time to address a particular task. We all know there are twenty-four hours in a day, and we are all busy, so it is not really correct when we say, "I am too busy." When I hear those words, I translate them into a roundabout admission that the task or meeting is not as important as the other things in that person's life. In fact, one way to discover a team member's lack of commitment to the process is his or her inability to schedule a meeting ninety days out.

Locations

In scheduling the next meeting, keep in mind that location is also important. I recommend scheduling all quarterly meetings off-site, if possible, because it is important to limit interruptions that can occur on the premises. Moreover, while it may seem like a minor detail, I strongly recommend that all electronic devices be turned off to limit distractions. The group can always take a break to check email and messages.

Subsequent Quarterly Meetings

Congratulations on getting this far in the succession planning process. Once you have gone through The Succession Solution℠, you want to be prepared for the next quarterly meeting. Prior to the scheduled meeting, reach out to each person who agreed to be responsible for the completion of an assigned task, and inquire how the task is proceeding. This will ensure your meeting is effective and productive.

You will find that a defined deadline is a great motivator. In *The 12 Week Year*, Moran states the he has found that "the top performers … are great, not because their ideas are better, but because their execution disciplines are better." I have found the same when using The Succession Solution℠. Usually around the second month, about a month before we are to meet, things start getting done.

When you meet with the people who agreed to take on quarter tasks, you may discover that they have made little or no progress. Don't be alarmed; there may be valid reasons for the task not being completed by the next quarterly meeting. If the task will not be completed, you will want to know why. You may determine that it was the wrong task, or you may need to dedicate more resources to the task. At this stage, you are trying to understand the status of the task, and whether or not the person needs additional help or you need to adjust the task identified at the last planning meeting.

The objective to scheduling this one-on-one prior to the next meeting is to better prepare the person for when all the stakeholders meet again, so they can provide greater insight on the effectiveness or utility of the task.

At the next quarterly meeting, you will begin by confirming that the first five stages of The Succession Solution℠ remain valid and do not need amended or adjusted. Once you confirm the basic plan is still valid, you will then have each person report on their assigned task.

Based on the status of the previously assigned task, you will then establish a new set of tasks to be completed by the next quarter.

I promise you that if you follow this process through at least four quarterly meetings, you will be surprised at how much you will accomplish in your ultimate vision of succession.

Quarterly Review	
18. 90 days	**Resp. Pty**
Management meets to discuss next CEO	
Existing CEO meets with financial planner for retirement	
Shareholders provide names of potential director	
19. Success Criteria • Management meets and has recommendations • Shareholders provide director name • CEO meets with financial planner	
20. Celebration of Success • Attend baseball game	**21. Next Meeting Date**

Keys to Chapter

1. Create a schedule and commit to meeting and reporting on a quarterly basis. Otherwise, the urgent will take the place of the important.

2. Decide from your annual goals which tasks to prioritize and work toward accomplishing in the next quarter that will move you closer to your annual goals.

3. Assign someone a task or tasks to report on at the next quarterly meeting. Make sure they have the resources and responsibility to accomplish that task.

4. Set the date and location of your next meeting at the end of each quarterly meeting.

5. Don't forget to celebrate!

Part IV: Conclusion

CHAPTER FIFTEEN: TAKING ACTION

"It is Not the Strongest of the Species that Survives but the Most Adaptable."

– Leon C. Megginson

Alfred Nobel was born into a family of engineers, and he too became an engineer and inventor. During Alfred's life, he registered hundreds of patents. However, it was the invention of dynamite that made him famous as well as wealthy. In today's dollars, Alfred's wealth at passing would approach 200 million dollars.

In an odd twist of fate, a blunder by a French newspaper is said to have changed how Alfred wanted to be remembered.[38] In 1888, this newspaper mistakenly printed Alfred's obituary when in fact it was his brother, Ludwig, who had passed away. Alfred's mistaken obituary called him "the merchant of death," and discussed the deadly impact of Alfred's invention, dynamite. Reading this article, Alfred may have decided he did not want to be remembered in this manner. As a result, much to the dissatisfaction of his family, co-workers, and even his country, he changed his will, leaving over 90 percent of his estate to the creation of a series of five prizes to be awarded "to those who, during the preceding year, shall have conferred the greatest benefit on mankind."

Similar to Ebenezer Scrooge, Alfred Nobel used his premature obituary to alter his future. My questions for you are these: How do you want to be remembered? How do you want to be remembered by your family, your employees, and your community?

In his book, *Legacy*, James Kerr states that true leaders are stewards of the future. They take responsibility for adding to the legacy of humanity. I wrote *The Succession Solution*^{SM} to help you find, establish, and execute your legacy, as it relates to your business. It provides you with the tools you need to develop your own roadmap, and it shows you how to get there. While your destination may be different from others, this book can help you reach it.

I encourage you to begin the succession planning process by defining the values and principles you want to instill and maintain in your company. Your values make up your culture. No rules, procedures, or regulations will do any good unless they are rooted in your business culture. During a crisis, you, your family, and your entire team will look to your values, principles, and overall culture to answer difficult questions. All-important stakeholders need to know your culture to ascertain what they can expect and whether or not they want to be a part of the organization.

Once you have established your purpose and culture, set your ultimate destination. Even though you may never achieve or reach your North Star, it will position and guide you in right direction. When your ultimate vision is established, answer "why" you want to complete your succession plan. Your "why" lays the foundation for your purpose. Your why is your reason for change, and if you can find a reason for change, you will have the strength to finish. I urge you then to look for those risks or obstacles that might be blocking your way. Remember, though, that until you know where you are going, you can't identify the obstacles. If there's a traffic jam north of the city and I am travelling south, I will not encounter a roadblock. Only after deciding where I am going can I look at the road ahead to plot the course and discover any detours I must follow to avoid delays.

Remember too that obstacles and threats, when seen through the right lens, can become opportunities. Once identified, you and your team will decide how to mitigate the obstacle and/or capitalize on the challenge. Being stuck in one place is a temporary position, not a destiny. The Succession Solution^{SM} not only helps you identify the risks, obstacles, and threats to your organization's succession plan, it helps you find solutions.

As you discover solutions to your threats and obstacles, decide how to attack those roadblocks by setting reasonable goals and timelines. There is always a process or timeline to follow. In succession planning, look at least three years ahead to decide what you want to accomplish within that time line to move closer to your vision of the future.

After establishing your three-year goals with objective criteria in place to determine their success or accomplishment, you will break the process into smaller more manageable parts. This is done by establishing one-year and, finally, quarterly goals.

With your quarterly goals in place, a very important step comes into play: action. Without action, your entire succession plan is but a dream. When you break your goals into quarterly action steps, you make them easier to accomplish, and the entire process becomes more manageable. Similarly, when you make a single person responsible for reporting on the status of each quarterly goal, the target will be met. In fact, you will be surprised by how fast your quarterly goals are accomplished when you assign them to one person. By giving the task to one person, it encourages them to take a team approach, since the team—and the plan—is relying on them.

Time to Act

With this book, you now have the tools you need to develop, implement, and complete your succession plan. As I have said throughout, you don't need The Succession Solution℠ to accomplish your succession planning goals. Any good process can work (even though I think The Succession Solution℠ is the most promising). I do want to emphasize in this closing moment, however, that the perfect succession plan does not exist, so don't waste your time searching for the Holy Grail of plans.

What's more, recognize from the outset that your succession planning process will not happen without challenge or conflict. I have never been involved in the accomplishment of a succession plan where conflict did not exist on some level. Indeed, positive change often is brought about by conflict, and your succession planning process is about change. One of the most important parts of the process will be how you manage, discuss, and resolve conflict, for this orientation will determine the ultimate success of your succession plan.

Once you go through this transition process, expect to gain other valuable benefits. You will likely find with the successful succession of your business you attain personal, family and even community goals you set for yourself.

Now is the time to act. Think about the smallest step you can take to move closer to implementing your succession plan. Discuss the matter with your spouse, partner, close family member, or any other important stakeholders in your life. I would also recommend that you try to speak to someone with succession planning expertise.

The next step is yours to take. I wish you great success with your plans!

> "Where we go from there is a choice I leave to you."
>
> The Matrix

About the Author

Bradley J. Franc, the creator of The Succession Solution℠, is an accomplished entrepreneur, business coach, strategist, business lawyer and CPA (inactive) who specializes in the transfer of family and closely-held businesses.

Brad began his professional career as a CPA, working for the international accounting firm now known as EY. From there, Brad became an entrepreneur, strategic business adviser and business lawyer representing every aspect of the closely-held business. He has formed four separate companies, two of which were named nine separate times to the prestigious INC Magazine Fastest Growing Companies in the USA list.

He has counseled hundreds of closely-held business owners on their business continuation and succession plans. He has been a board member for a number of both for-profit and non-profit organizations including Fort Pitt Fund, Global Tax Management, General Carbide, The University of Pittsburgh, WISH Foundation, and LaRoche University.

Brad was named by Worth Magazine as one of the top 100 attorneys in the United States and has appeared nationally on Fox News and Bloomberg Television. Brad's articles have been cited by the Supreme Court of the U.S., and he has also written and been published in numerous professional journals and publications including Forbes and U.S. News & World Report.

For further information, contact The Succession Coach LLC at www.thesuccessionsolution.com.

You can reach the author at bradfranc@thesuccessionsolution.com

ENDNOTES

[1] Pamela Weintraub, "The Doctor Who Drank Infectious Broth, Gave Himself an Ulcer, and Solved a Medical Mystery," *Discover*, April 8, 2010, http://discovermagazine.com/2010/mar/07-dr-drank-broth-gave-ulcer-solved-medical-mystery.

[2] "World's Oldest Family Inn's Secret to Succession," KPMG, posted December 5, 2016, https://home.kpmg.com/xx/en/home/insights/2016/12/worlds-oldest-family-inns-secret-succession.html.

[3] Dan Roam, The Back of the Napkin: Solving Problems and Selling Ideas with Pictures (New York: Portfolio, 2008).

[4] Adrian Wooldridge, "To Have and to Hold: Family Companies," special report, *The Economist*, April 18, 2015, http://www.economist.com/sites/default/files/20150418_family.pdf.

[5] Elizabeth Arias and Jiaquan Xu, "United States Life Tables, 2015," *National Vital Statistics Reports* 67, no. 7 (November 13, 2018): 47, table 19, https://www.cdc.gov/nchs/data/nvsr/nvsr67/nvsr67_07-508.pdf.

[6] Internal Revenue Service, *SOI Tax Stats at a Glance* (2018), https://www.irs.gov/system/files/irs-soi/18taxstatscard.pdf; Craig Doidge et al., "Eclipse of the Public Corporation or Eclipse of the Public Markets?," (NBER Working Paper no. 24265, National Bureau of Economic Research, Cambridge, MA, January 2018), https://doi.org/10.3386/w24265, and *Journal of Applied Corporate Finance* 30, no. 1 (March 1, 2018): 8–16, https://doi.org/10.1111/jacf.12272.

[7] Aileron, "The Facts Of Family Business," Forbes, July 31, 2013, https://www.forbes.com/sites/aileron/2013/07/31/the-facts-of-family-business/.

8 "Keeping the Family Business Healthy, John Ward January 2011, https://www.familybusinessinstitute.com/consulting/succession-planning/.

[9] Roy Williams and Vic Preisser, *Preparing Heirs: Five Steps to a Successful Transition of Family Wealth and Values* (San Francisco, CA: Robert Reed, 2010), 35–49.

[10] Williams and Preisser, *Preparing Heirs*, 31.

[11] Williams and Preisser, *Preparing Heirs*, 33.

12 PwC, *The Missing Middle: Bridging the Strategy Gap* in US Family Firms, 2017 US Family Business Survey, https://www.pwc.com/us/en/private-company-services/publications/assets/pwc-family-business-survey-us-2017.pdf, 14-15.

[13] Marvin Cruz, *Getting the Transition Right: Survey Results on Small Business Succession Planning* (Canadian Federation of Independent Business, 2018), https://www.cfib-fcei.ca/sites/default/files/2018-11/Getting-the-transition-right-succession-planning-report.pdf, 6-7.

[14] Vikram Bhalla and Nicolas Kachaner, *Succeeding with Succession Planning in Family Businesses: The Ten Key Principles* (Boston Consulting Group, 2015), http://image-src.bcg.com/Images/Succeeding_with_Succession_Mar_2015_tcm30-78046.pdf, 1-2.

[15] "Habit 3: Put First Things First," in Stephen R. Covey, *The 7 Habits of Highly Effective People: Powerful Lessons in Personal Change* (New York: Simon & Schuster, 2004).

[16] David Cay Johnston, "Dozens of Rich Americans Join In Fight to Retain the Estate Tax," *New York Times*, February 14, 2001, sec. U.S., https://www.nytimes.com/2001/02/14/us/dozens-of-rich-americans-join-in-fight-to-retain-the-estate-tax.html.

[17] *Merriam-Webster*, s.v. "community," accessed December 12, 2018, https://www.merriam-webster.com/dictionary/community.

[18] Christian Caspar, Ana Karina Dias, and Heinz-Peter Elstrodt, "The Five Attributes of Enduring Family Businesses," *McKinsey Quarterly* (January 2010), https://www.mckinsey.com/business-functions/organization/our-insights/the-five-attributes-of-enduring-family-businesses.

[19] Steve Hargreaves, "The richest Americans in history," *CNNMoney*, June 2, 2014, https://money.cnn.com/gallery/luxury/2014/06/01/richest-americans-in-history/index.html.

[20] "Elway, the first player taken in the 1983 college draft, did not have a bad game for his professional debut. A short game, maybe. He played only the first half because of a sore elbow and completed 1 of 8 passes, a 14-yarder to Rick Upchurch in the first quarter… 'It's difficult to be a great college quarterback and step right into the pros and do it,' [DeBerg] said. 'John still has things to learn. When he does, we'll be a better football team.'" Michael Janofsky, "Broncos Edge Steelers, 14-10," *New York Times*, September 5, 1983, sec. Sports, https://www.nytimes.com/1983/09/05/sports/broncos-edge-steelers-14-10.html.

[21] Brian O'Keefe, "Leadership Lessons from Alabama Football Coach Nick Saban," *Fortune*, September 7, 2012, http://fortune.com/2012/09/07/leadership-lessons-from-alabama-football-coach-nick-saban/.

[22] Anthony Greenbank, *The Book of Survival* (New York: Harper & Row, 1967).

[23] William George Jordan, *The Power of Purpose* (New York: Fleming H. Revell, 1910), 12.

[24] "Passing On the Crown: Family Businesses," *The Economist*, Nov 4, 2004, https://www.economist.com/special-report/2004/11/04/passing-on-the-crown.

[25] Claudio Fernández-Aráoz, Sonny Iqbal, and Jörg Ritter, "Leadership Lessons

from Great Family Businesses," *Harvard Business Review*, April 1, 2015, https://hbr.org/2015/04/leadership-lessons-from-great-family-businesses.

[26] Proverbs 29:18 (King James Version).

[27] Dan Sullivan. *The Gap and the Gain: Building Your Progress and Happiness Entirely on How Your Brain Works for You* (Toronto: The Strategic Coach, 2017), https://s3.amazonaws.com/strategic-coach-marketing-assets/downloads/GapAndGainDownload.pdf.

[28] As paraphrased by Viktor Frankl in *Man's Search for Meaning* (1946).

[29] Simon Sinek, *Start with Why: How Great Leaders Inspire Everyone to Take Action* (New York: Penguin, 2011).

[30] Ryan Holiday, *The Obstacle Is the Way: The Timeless Art of Turning Trials into Triumph* (New York: Penguin, 2014), 158.

[31] Quoted by Ryan Holiday, *The Obstacle Is the Way*, 3.

[32] Williams and Preisser, *Preparing Heirs*, 43.

[33] Williams and Preisser, *Preparing Heirs*, 48.

[34] Dwight D. Eisenhower, "Address at the Second Assembly of the World Council of Churches, Evanston, Illinois, August 19, 1954," The American Presidency Project, https://www.presidency.ucsb.edu/node/232572.

[35] John M. Broder, "Schwarzkopf's War Plan Based on Deception," *Los Angeles Times*, February 28, 1991, http://articles.latimes.com/1991-02-28/news/mn-2834_1_war-plan.

[36] Nitin Nohria, William Joyce, and Bruce Roberson, "What Really Works," *Harvard Business Review*, July 2003, https://hbr.org/2003/07/what-really-works.

[37] Stephen R. Covey, *How to Develop Your Personal Mission Statement* (Grand Harbor Press, 2013), loc. 19 of 484, Kindle.

[38] Evan Andrews, "Did a Premature Obituary Inspire the Nobel Prize?," *History.com*, December 9, 2016, https://www.history.com/news/did-a-premature-obituary-inspire-the-nobel-prize.

APPENDIX

The Succession Solution[SM] Completed Worksheet Example

Purpose

1. What are the Core Principles of Stakeholders?

- Integrity
- Provide top quality service
- Respect employees like customers—everyone is family

2. What is the Ultimate Succession Plan Vision? (Find your North Star)

- A new CEO, fully accepted by management and board of directors; ownership, effectively leading the company

3. Why? (Does Vision Align with Core Principles?)

- To ensure the continued success of the Company for the shareholders, employees and community

4. What Does Failure Look Like?

- No support for next generation of leaders, causing family discord and loss of Company value

Discovery

5. Where are we now and what is in place for succession?

(Where is the Red Dot?)

(Management, Ownership, Employees, Family Dynamics)

- Shareholders' Agreement in place
- Management correctly in place
- No plan for next CEO

Challenge

6. Strengths

- Financially strong
- Name recognition in industry
- Good relationship with key customers

7. Opportunities

- Time to decide on next CEO
- New CEO could begin to develop new customer relationships

8. Obstacles

- Family discord on who should be next CEO
- Key customers have close relationship with current CEO

9. Strategies for Overcoming Obstacles

- Have management explain to family CEO recommendations
- Have family member explain who and why they want this CEO
- Have existing CEO begin to introduce next CEO to key customers

Reporter: ____________________ **Meeting Date:** ____________________

| Business Name: _____ | Business Activity: _____ |
| Initiation Date: _____ | |

Mission (3 Years)	Annual Review	Quarterly Review	
10. Goals	**14. Goals**	**18. 90 days**	**Resp. Pty**
• Next CEO in place • Prior CEO transfer to Chairman of the Board • Board created with various family members	• Management provides CEO recommendations • Shareholders' consensus on new Board member • Develop CEO role and compensation plan	Management meets to discuss next CEO	
		Existing CEO meets with financial planner for retirement	
		Shareholders provide names of potential director	
11. Obstacles	**15. Obstacles**		
• Existing CEO needs retirement package • Existing Board resistant to change • Family shareholders don't agree on next CEO	• Inactive Board • CEO uncertain about financial situation • Shareholder discord		
12. Actions	**16. Actions**	**19. Success Criteria**	
• Create retirement package for existing CEO • Shareholders consensus as to new Board • Board hires next CEO • New independent BOD member added	• Meet with management regarding CEO • CEO meets with financial planner • List key customer relationships with CEO	• Management meets and has recommendations • Shareholders provide director name • CEO meets with financial planner	
13. Measurements of Success (KPIs)	**17. Measurements of Success (KPIs)**	**20. Celebration of Success**	
• Board meetings working on succession plan • New CEO in place • Retirement plan completed	• Shareholders agree to new Board • List of key customers provided with a transition plan to introduce prospective CEO	• Attend baseball game	
		21. Next Meeting Date	

Download a printable version of this worksheet at **www.thesuccessionsolution.com/workbook**.

Made in the USA
Columbia, SC
19 September 2020

21074829R00126